G000114191

Effective Screen Reading
Manage E-mail and the Internet
More Efficiently

Tarmo Toikka

HRD Press, Inc. • **Amherst** • **Massachusetts**

Copyright © 2008, Tarmo Toikka

All rights reserved. No part of this publication may be reproduced, stored in a retrieval system, or transmitted in any form or by any means, electronic, mechanical, photocopying, recording or otherwise without the permission of the publisher.

Published by: HRD Press, Inc.
                 22 Amherst Road
                 Amherst, Massachusetts 01002
                 1-800-822-2801 (U.S. and Canada)
                 413-253-3488
                 413-253-3490 (fax)
                 www.hrdpress.com

ISBN 978-1-59996-111-8

Production services by Jean Miller
Editorial services by Sally Farnham
Cover design by Eileen Klockars

To my precious family, and especially to our children in their lifelong learning experience.

Contents

Effective Screen Reading

Foreword

Today, young people increasingly spend more time with computers. Jyrki J. Kasvi recognizes the differences in generations of users of technology based on the generations of the systems that had introduced them to the world of digital technologies. Mr. Kasvi, now a member of the Finnish Parliament, considers himself part of the Commodore 64 generation, while the PlayStation 2 generation is today studying at universities and utilizing e-learning in their studies. This group learned the basics of digital media before adolescence, with many learning it before elementary school. Using a nonlinear approach and being confident with several parallel processes and roles are some of the characteristics of those youngsters who have spent their childhood chatting and playing at their computers. At school, they have been taught media-literacy: how to read books, movies, video, multimedia, and the Web. At home, they demonstrate the principles of intergenerational informal learning while intuitively helping their parents with the complicated user-interfaces of various gadgets. When they enter working life, they have mastered the citizens' skills of the Knowledge Society on a level that their pre-Commodore 64 generation parents could only have dreamed of. Will it be enough, and does this scenario apply to the majority of Europe or only to a small number of techies in Finland?

Since 2000, the European Union has increased its activities addressing the challenges of the Knowledge Society to improve learning and to develop skills. The eEurope Action Plans have put e-learning and e-skills high on the political agenda. Effective screen reading is emerging as a new key competence required by workers and citizens of the Knowledge Society. The 2004–2007 e-Learning Programme, research projects on technology enhanced learning in the IST programme, projects in the eTEN programme, as well as projects in the European Social Fund 2000–2006, have demonstrated how e-learning helps create new forms of learning within the education and training systems at work and in society at large. The launch of the i2010 and Lifelong Learning Programme will provide renewed impetus to the efforts to use information and communication technology (ICT) to improve learning, help workers acquire key skills, and support society to become more inclusive.

Despite the considerable efforts undertaken, there are many open questions surrounding the use of ICT and the skills needed to participate in the Knowledge Society. Skills have a considerable role to play in workers' adaptability and employability. Europe's ability to remain competitive, achieve higher employment, and ensure future economic growth requires more effective investment in human capital through better education and training. ICT has a considerable role to play in achieving this, especially by means of increasing access and flexibility in education and training. Effective screen reading is a fundamental element when improving competitiveness and supporting inclusion in the Knowledge Society. Ensuring that everyone has the necessary skills, competence, experiences, and attitudes to make effective use of ICT is probably the biggest challenge of the Knowledge Society development.

The PlayStation 2 generation has mastered several of the competencies required for effective screen reading. Having a nonlinear approach to media and being confident with several parallel processes and roles, as well as having the capability to intuitively use various hardware and software and connect to the networks, are all components of the competency profile for effective screen reading. In addition, personal knowledge management skills are needed: how to search, retrieve, edit, store, and publish information and how to identify meaningful pieces of information in the oceans of information available. Time and work-flow management skills are valuable when surviving the information overflow. Being digitally literate, we should also be aware of and respect the intellectual property rights and understand the ethical issues related to ICT and digital media. Collaboration is present in almost everything we do when using ICT, thus emphasizing the importance of communication skills as a component of effective screen reading. Reading skills and understanding the ergonomics of human machine interfaces contribute to effective screen reading. The list seems endless, at least when taking the holistic knowledge society perspective to effective screen reading. The majority of related information sources available limit their approach according to the levels of educational systems (e.g., effective screen reading in elementary school) or desired competency profiles (e.g., various computer driver's license schemes), and a plethora of guidebooks and manuals are dedicated to specific services (e.g., public services online).

Effective Screen Reading is a welcome addition to the new category of books on effective screen reading. It covers several branches of the large tree of effective screen reading. It serves the needs of all pre-Commodore 64 generations while including valuable hints for experienced users of ICT on how to increase the effectiveness of everyday work processes.

Espoo
October 2006

Tapio Koskinen
Senior Advisor
Helsinki University of Technology

Acknowledgments

First of all, I would like to show my appreciation to my loving wife, Minna, for the trust she has had in me during all these years when *Effective Screen Reading* was under development. Without her support, this book would have never materialized. Also our children, Miikka, Minttu, and Marissa, have been most understanding for all the nights when their father has been awake typing the text. The only family members not bothered by my work have been our dogs, Blanca and Tipsu.

A special thanks goes to my very good friend and neighbor, David Lindop, who has offered several comments and ideas to improve the text. He has also done a fabulous job proofreading the book. Thanks also to HRD Press and Robert W. Carkhuff for accepting to publish *Effective Screen Reading,* and to Sally Farnham for editing the book for the U.S. market.

Fuengirola, Spain
November 2007

Tarmo Toikka

CBE Consulting S.L.
Calle Castaño 51, Fuengirola 29640 Spain
Tel. +34-670 87 34 90, Fax: +34-952 19 60 65
E-mail: tarmo.toikka@screen-smart.com
Web: www.screen-smart.com

Introduction

Dozens of books have been written about how to use traditional speed, rapid, and power reading techniques for printed material. *Effective Screen Reading* is the first book to address fast and effective reading and learning *directly* to computer screens. You will find various books on the market explaining how to use browsers, search engines, and e-mail systems from a technical viewpoint. However, our primary goal in writing this book was to focus on the most important techniques that will offer significant value in managing information and achieving results in the midst of the electronic information explosion.

Effective Screen Reading is about implementing tried and tested principles of on-screen productivity and effectiveness with a computer screen. Many ideas in this book have been developed by the author while training businesspeople in leading companies around Europe to increase their productivity with computers. We have seen many participants in our training sessions take our techniques and develop them further to suit their own particular needs and business requirements. We are confident that this book will become a springboard to help *you* be more productive and effective.

Reading electronic text, e-mails, and Web pages on a computer screen does not follow the same principles as reading the same material printed on paper. Various technical factors pose a true challenge for the human eye and make reading much more difficult. On average, reading text on a computer screen—*screen reading*—can be as much as 30 percent slower with less comprehension than reading printed text. Perhaps this is the reason why so many people prefer to make a printout from the text they see on the screen.

Objectives

Effective Screen Reading has four main objectives:

1. Offer concrete techniques that will enable you to speed read e-mails and other documents directly from the computer screen. You will develop your digital reading ability in order to increase your understanding of what you have read, remember it longer, and communicate it with clarity and speed.

2. Improve your speed to knowledge by finding the information you want faster from the mass of electronic data presented.

3. Develop easy-to-use techniques to select, scan, understand, and remember key messages. These techniques will significantly improve your productivity and help you manage your e-mail system and the Internet more effectively.

4. Take into consideration your working environment, especially the ergonomic factors, in order to reduce work-related stress.

Organization of Chapters

In order to assist you in reading this book more efficiently, we have divided it into five main chapters and a summary. Efficiency means that you understand what you are reading, remember it longer, and start actively using digital reading techniques in your everyday work. Each chapter in *Effective Screen Reading* contains the following three elements to help you achieve your objectives:

- **The preview.** The preview sets the goals for the chapter and briefly describes the main topics to be covered. This type of overview at the beginning of the chapter provides you with the big picture. Consequently, it becomes much easier to understand the chapter more quickly as you combine the new information presented in the book with your existing knowledge.

- **The chapter itself.** The chapter and its sub-chapters give answers to the established goals by presenting the necessary techniques and other pertinent information for managing on-screen data.

- **The summary and onward.** The summary highlights the main topics presented and acts as a bridge by linking the contents of each chapter to the next one. Here one might recall Leonardo da Vinci´s famous saying that "everything connects to everything else." Onward will then set the scene for the next chapter.

Exercises: Reading, Relaxation, and Vision

Traditional speed reading books contain various exercises, many of which may sometimes make the reader tired and result in a lower understanding of actual text. We have included only six reading exercises (plus the one measuring your current reading speed and comprehension, each lasting one minute). By limiting the number of exercises to only six, we have reduced the number of pages in this book. This makes *Effective Screen Reading* an easy-to-handle quick-reference guide.

Each exercise has a specific purpose. The text for all the exercises has been carefully selected in order to provide you information about various topics.

In addition to the set exercises in this book, it is essential that you practice both often and regularly, and we suggest you do this in front of your computer monitor at work or at home. You can also do all the reading exercises directly from your computer monitor at the HRD Press Web site (www.hrdpress.com/effectivescreenreading/ exercises. html).

For increased concentration, *Effective Screen Reading* contains five different types of relaxation exercises, each lasting only one minute. Furthermore, the book has pyramidal and other types of exercises to train your vision capacity.

— 1 —
World of Electronic Information

In this chapter, you will discover the benefits you can realize when you use all your brainpower while reading. A new technique—SuperBrowse—will show you how to read and understand the *Effective Screen Reading* book in only a few minutes. Since you may want to read and practice all this material on your screen, we will show you how to do this also. At the end of the chapter, we will briefly discuss strategic values of today's learning organization.

In today's society of informatics, people constantly face new challenges. The speed of change in the environment has been extremely rapid, especially in the past ten years. The excess of available information—*the information glut*—has made all types of forecasts on new developments extremely difficult to predict. To understand this concept, imagine that you are on a train, the speed of which is constantly accelerating. The landscapes outside are becoming more and more blurred as the speed of the train increases. It gets to the point where all you can see are the seats and the other passengers—the rest is just a blur. You seem to have lost your ability to know where you are and in which direction you are heading.

The main reason for this increased speed of change in the environment can be attributed to the spreading of computers and their universal network called the Internet or the Web. This worldwide network of computers has created a flood of information. It contains hundreds of billions of pages of various types of information available to everyone instantly. It also offers the possibility for rapid communication by allowing anyone to send and receive electronic mail.

For the past 10 to 15 years, experts have predicted the transition to the paperless office. We are sure you will agree from your experience in today's workplace that the paperless office is only a myth, and that in reality the complete opposite is true. Paper consumption continues to spiral upward, not down, while the surplus of available information keeps piling up.

It has been estimated that scientific information doubles every 12 years, other information every two years. A report published by *Reuters* (2001) shows that over the past 30 years, more data have been produced than in the preceding 10,000 years, with over a thousand books a day being published. Scientists at the University of California, Berkeley, go even further with their predictions on the information glut: they estimate that during the next few years, mankind will produce as much information as it has produced since records began!

Habits, Beliefs, and Delusions: The Story of the Samasu-Indians

Let us start with a story that relates perfectly to the common delusions in reading and the interpretation of information. In the late 1980s, a rapid epidemic of leprosy spread through the jungles of the Brazilian Amazon and hit hardest a rare, almost extinct tribe of the Samasu-Indians. The Brazilian government decided to ask for help from a private clinic in Stockholm, Sweden.

At that time, this clinic had the most knowledgeable specialists in treating leprous patients, and a mission of experts was sent from Sweden to the jungles of the Amazon. They were carrying a very potent medicine in the form of small pills known to cure leprosy almost immediately. Having arrived in Belém, a city in the northern part of Brazil, they took a primitive raft on the Amazon River, heading toward the jungle. When they arrived at the little village of the Samasu-Indians, they were confronted with an insurmountable obstacle: there was no one who knew how to communicate with the tribe, since its native language was extremely rare. Hardly anyone outside the tribe understood it.

Luckily the mission leader had a brilliant idea: "Let's draw pictures showing what to do with the pills!"

It seemed to be a fantastic idea, since obviously everybody understands the language of pictures. So they sketched out three posters, which they staked into the ground (see Figure 1.1). In the first poster, they drew a bottle containing red miracle pills and the face of a leprous Indian. In the second picture, they sketched an arrow from the bottle to the mouth of the suffering Indian. The third poster showed an empty bottle and a face of a happy Samasu-Indian. The pictures were posted around various places in the village. The Swedish rescue team went back to their tent and waited for the Indians to line up for the pills.

However, the tribe returned painted in war colors. With their sharp spears, they attacked the Swedish mission and forced them to run away. The doctors were most amazed. What had gone wrong?

They investigated the matter and were finally given the answer by an expert in Indian tribes found in São Paulo.

The answer was quite simple: the tribe of the Samasu-Indians reads from right to left.

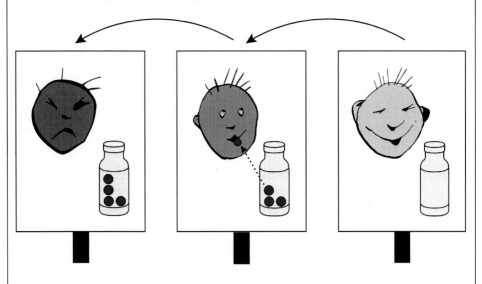

Figure 1.1: The story of the Samasu-Indians.

The story above clearly demonstrates how easy it is to make a mistake when you rely on your old habits and use them as such in a totally new situation. The same applies to the computer screen, which constitutes a totally new situation for reading and a true challenge for the human eyes and brain. By adhering to your traditional reading techniques, you will severely limit your speed and comprehension. To overcome this problem, you need to set the reference point for your reading speed and understanding, which we will cover at the end of this chapter.

Effective Screen Reading: What does this mean?

A definition of a "digitally literate" person is one who can manage vast amounts of electronic information efficiently.

Effective screen reading includes the individual's capability to:

- Manage efficiently the electronic flow of messages and information directly on the monitor, and only print what is required.

- Set reading goals and vary reading speed on a computer screen, depending on the type of material and time available.

- Achieve maximum benefit from the time invested in reading e-mail, the Internet, and other forms of electronic information.

- Use Internet search engines effectively to find the required information in the shortest possible time and, consequently, increase the time available for undertaking other tasks such as decision making and analysis.

- Know the natural movement of the human eye on the screen and make use of this information for more efficient reading.

- Reduce work-related stress by taking into consideration ergonomic factors when working at computer workstations.

To achieve all this, you need to maximize the use of both brain and vision capacity. It is imperative to adopt proper techniques to find the required information in the shortest possible time, to read and understand its contents quickly, and to use it for the right purpose. However, if you give up using your imaginative powers, reduce the time for daydreaming, and limit visualization on subject matters, the natural functioning of the brain will be restricted, resulting in the brain literally starting to "die." The solution to overcoming this dilemma is the concept of *whole brain reading*. Whole brain reading releases your "hidden" speed reading ability, which is needed to efficiently manage electronic information. This ability is needed to read both computer screens and printed matter in order for you to become a truly efficient reader in the 21st century of informatics. The principal idea is that in order to prevent the brain from "dying," you need to harness all its available capacities and abilities.

When reading text on a computer screen, most people use the same traditional techniques that they apply when reading books or printouts. These techniques have been taught either at school, or they have been learned and adopted without any guidance. Actually, there are many habits and beliefs strongly implanted in people's minds on how reading should be done, and these methods are also applied directly to the text seen on the computer screen.

The change from an ordinary reader to the *whole brain reader*—who can easily manage the plethora of electronic information—does not happen overnight. You shouldn't expect miracles. The development process will be gradual and will require some efforts and exercise on your part. The exercises in this book have been designed to support this gradual process. However, the practice does not require any specially reserved time in your schedule, since it can be carried out every day at your computer screen during working or studying hours. With your busy schedule, this is obviously a relief. So relax and enjoy yourself as your reading speed gets faster and your understanding gets better.

Reading Speed and Understanding

The following statistics may surprise and hopefully reassure you. The average reading rate for adults is somewhere around 180 to 240 words per minute in printed matter (see Figure 1.2).

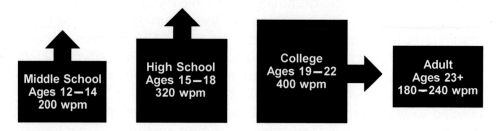

Figure 1.2: Reading speeds in different age groups (wpm = words per minute).

The decline in words per minute in adults is for the most part due to lack of practice. Reading speed is like a muscle. To keep it fit, you have to use it. The amount of reading done after graduation is far less than the volume undertaken as a student. Multiple tests performed with businesspeople in different countries have proven that the actual speeds (before any training is carried out) vary from 150 to 250 words per minute with 40 to 60 percent understanding.

Due to the complexity of the computer screen, the reading speeds of electronic texts are on average 20 to 30 percent slower than reading the same text on paper. What this means is that the screen reading rates for adults vary between just 105 and 175 wpm. It is therefore no wonder that many of us prefer to print e-mails and Web pages for more convenient and faster reading.

Evaluating Your Level of Understanding

Contrary to books about traditional speed reading techniques, this book does not include multiple choice test questions to measure comprehension of each reading exercise. Your best evaluation is to monitor your understanding subjectively. What matters is how the new information supports and connects to your existing knowledge. Understanding is defined by how well you comprehend the text *while reading*. This self-evaluation has four levels of understanding:

- Very well (understanding over 75 percent)
- Well (understanding 50 to 75 percent)
- Sufficiently (understanding 25 to 50 percent)
- Little (understanding less than 25 percent)

The curve in Figure 1.3 clearly illustrates how most people compare in understanding. The average adult reads around 200 words per minute and comprehends more or less 50 percent of the text. Use the percentages in the figure to compare your understanding with others.

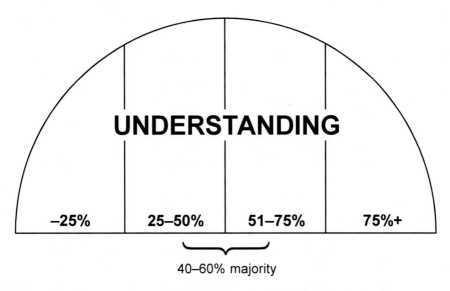

Figure 1.3: Average understanding (in percentages) of a textbook among adults.

Comprehension means understanding what you are reading at a certain moment from the screen. It is a highly complex situation. There are many factors that influence understanding:

- Your ability to concentrate on the subject matter. This depends greatly on the working environment (lighting, disturbances), your emotions, physical comfort (ergonomics), and attitude toward the subject matter.

- The difficulty of the subject matter.

- Your previous knowledge, motivation, and curiosity about the subject matter.

- The type style, the use of colors, and the layout of the Web page being read.

The general opinion is that the faster you read, the less you understand. Of course *if* this is true, there wouldn't be any reason to speed read since you obviously want to comprehend the text you are going through.

You will find out in Chapters 2 and 3 if the general opinion is correct or not.

SuperBrowse: Learn this Book in 12 Minutes

How can you effectively go through this book in 12 minutes, if that is all the time you can spare?

People with an academic degree read on average after graduation only one professional book or textbook per year. Why so few?

Going back to your school days, there were probably many times when you read a textbook and did not fully understand what it was all about. However, reading these required textbooks was necessary to pass an exam. Once the test was over, you most likely moved on and started to study a new subject from scratch for the next examination. It was probably hard and frustrating work, since you were learning unsound study habits. No one tells you the important fact about learning: the more you learn and remember, the easier it is to learn more. The brain, like any other muscle in the human body, needs regular exercise, and *continuous learning* is its workout program. Once you stop exercising your brain, your reading ability deteriorates.

It is always easy to find an excuse not to read books, for example, saying that reading would take up too much of your valuable time. However, friends and colleagues at work may suggest interesting books that can develop you professionally. You buy these books and they end up at the office or on the bookshelf at home. However, nowadays the contents of these books can also be found in an electronic form (on a CD-ROM, downloaded from the Internet, etc.) to be read as e-books from the screen or from a handheld.

Often they contain information relevant to your business, and reading them would be to your advantage. You know this but just don't find the time to read them, and consequently they become a stress factor. These books, or more importantly unread business information, dominate your life instead of you dominating the information. So what could be the solution?

The solution is to use a technique called *SuperBrowse* that can help you master all this information. This book has about 200 pages, and you need only 5 minutes to go through the main points. To master and remember the main issues presented, you need to invest about 12 minutes total. As an exercise, we recommend you SuperBrowse this book. Take a look at the steps presented, follow them closely, and use them immediately. You will be amazed how fast you can actually comprehend the main points. By browsing the material, you can make the very important decisions regarding the following:

- Is it worthwhile reading the whole book in-depth?

- Do some chapters contain information so valuable that you should spend more time reading these parts first?

Five Steps in SuperBrowsing Effective Screen Reading

Just for a moment, clear your mind of everything you have learned previously on how to read a new book. You should have available paper, pen or pencil, and small bookmarks.

1. Take a look at the title of this book—*Effective Screen Reading*. For a few minutes, think about what you know about the subject, and jot down your thoughts on paper, allowing flow of random associations as they come into your mind. This technique is called *Applied Imagination* (see Chapter 2), and it allows you to fasten any new information more easily to the existing knowledge that you posses on the topic.

2. Having completed Applied Imagination, take the book in your hands and hold it in a relaxed way. Leaf through your book by turning over the pages and looking at each briefly. Do not stop reading and spend no more than a few seconds on each page. Try to figure out how the book is put together

and what kind of *rhythm* it has. Is there a list of *contents*? How is it divided in *chapters* and *sub-chapters?* Does it contain *summaries, graphs, key points, keywords, pictures*? Is there an *index*, what information does it give, and does it bring something to your mind? What parts "jump out" and attract your eyes by being conspicuous?

3. Insert your bookmarks into those pages that look especially interesting, unusual, or remarkable in order to explore them later. Go through the book rhythmically. Keep to the 5-minute time limit.

4. Write a brief summary on the key messages in the book from *your* point of view. Refer back to those pages where you inserted bookmarks and investigate what has attracted your eyes. This is an excellent place to use a Mind Map® for the summary (please refer to Chapter 3). Use a maximum of 5 minutes to write down the summary.

5. Make a short presentation (2 minutes) on the main points to a friend or colleague (or to the mirror).

By using SuperBrowse, you can now make two decisions:

1. Did you get enough information? Do you now understand the contents sufficiently to allow you to place your summary in the book for future reference? Do you master the main points of the book? Or

2. Do you want to devote extra time and read the whole book or some sections of it in-depth since you now realize that it contains information important or valuable to you?

Whatever decision you make, you have already managed the information contained in the rest of the book. Congratulations! And it took 12 minutes in total.

SuperBrowse is an excellent way to master long texts. The equivalent term for electronic material is *DigiBrowse*, which is explained in Chapter 5. This technique is suitable for electronic books (e-books) that represent multiple media.

Single Medium vs. Multiple Media

The word *multimedia* is often used in learning and training. Other popular terms include *distance learning, computer-based training* using CD-ROMs, *video teleconference,* and *electronic performance support system.* This book in its printed version is regarded as *single medium* (simple technology) in contrast to *multimedia* (complex technology). The latter would be represented by the electronic version (electronic books, or e-books) of mostly the same material. Single medium requires that you, the reader, experience one format of information at a time. Thus, reading this subject in the form of a book would be a single medium experience. One might even call it "print" experience. The same applies when following a lecture, which is a single medium "classroom" experience. However, true multimedia allow for a constant mix of sounds, symbols, animation, text, and video, harnessing both sides of the brain and appealing to more than one of the five senses.

E-paper and E-books. Rapid development is taking place in the area of hardware for managing and reading electronic information. Commercial versions of e-books are available, which contain text from hundreds of printed books, totaling thousands of pages. These units are lightweight and portable. First versions of electronic paper, or e-paper, have also been developed at the Massachusetts Institute of Technology (MIT). This e-paper screen can be reloaded multiple times and currently has a thickness of 8 mm with a capacity of 100 pages, but continuous development ensures that physical size will be diminished, while the capacity will increase.

When reading text from the screen, the reader takes it for granted that the computer hardware and software are functioning perfectly. However, it is important to bear in mind the difference between printed and electronic text. This difference is best conveyed by Murphy's law (modified slightly by the author). Remember these when dealing with computers:

- Anything is possible if you don't know what you are reading about.
- Every solution breeds a new problem.

- Nothing is as easy as it looks.
- Everything takes longer than you think.
- Anything that can go wrong will go wrong.
- There is always somebody willing to find a solution, tomorrow.

The Success Formula for the Learning Organization

More and more attention is being focused on the management of knowledge in companies. Key areas in this information management include the following:

- the storage of available internal data
- the proper use of intellectual know-how of employees

To provide a few examples on how the requirements of data storage capacity have increased during the past few years, we can refer to the changes that have taken place at Northern Trust Corporation in Chicago and Stanford University. Northern Trust (a supplier of mainframe systems) has been trying to do more with less as data storage requirements have exploded from 1TB (terabyte = one thousand gigabytes) of capacity in 1999 to more than 40TB in a storage-area network (SAN) as of spring 2002. That figure topped 300TB in 2006 and is expected to grow to 500TB by 2009—an unbelievable expansion in only a few years. Another good example comes from the Stanford Linear Accelerator Center at Stanford University, whose database recently passed the 500TB mark, making it one of the largest in the world. The database began storing data in 1999. The 500TB of data in the database, if printed out, would fill 1 billion books. That's nearly 60 times the number of books in the Library of Congress, one of the largest public reference libraries in the world.

In addition to managing data storage, companies must also tap the intellectual know-how of employees to the fullest extent in order to be successful and survive in the global market. Typically companies do not use this wealth of knowledge, despite its potential influence on the improvement of business operations if made available to everyone in the organization. The fact is that more efficient use of collective knowledge will give a competitive advantage to businesses. To become a true learning organization, the company must clearly specify its strategic values and benefit from techniques such as SuperBrowse and Mind Mapping®.

Strategic Values

One way to analyze companies is to use a three-axis model reflecting the strategic values of a company. Three areas can be distinguished:

1. **Excellence in operations.** This is a combination of superior quality, very low costs, and the confidence that customers are showing toward the price and service offered by the company.

2. **Strong relationships with customers.** The main objective is to create, maintain, and develop good and close relations with customers on a long-term basis. Long-term value (LTV) of customers is the most important strategic consideration.

3. **Leadership in products.** For the majority of companies, the goal is to continually create new services and develop new products by using the latest technology. These new items must have superior quality and characteristics in order to be competitive on the market. The leadership in products strategy often requires that the company know how to "creatively destroy" old products when new innovations are launched to the market.

Figure 1.4 presents the strategic frames for two hypothetical companies A and B. The performance of these companies can be analyzed and measured in all three areas.

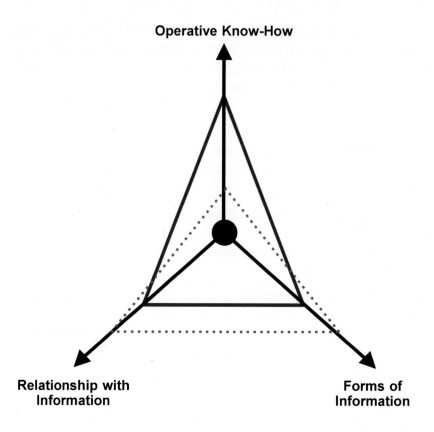

(Source: Forum Criticum, 1995)

Figure 1.4: A three-axis model on strategic values.

Each strategy alternative can be quantified and measured by looking at the following:

- business processes
- the organizational structure
- the management system
- the business culture of the company

Quantitative objectives can then be set, and the development in each area can be measured. This type of analysis gives a good basis for further strategy development.

Intellectual Capital

When referring to intellectual capital—or colloquially "know-how"—three strategic areas can be distinguished:

1. **Operative know-how.** One of the fundamental objectives in knowledge management is to change the company to become a learning organization. This type of company uses the operative know-how of its employees to benefit the whole unit. However, the organization and its employees need tangible tools to achieve this objective. Basic psychological processes play a very important role together with learning tools. The following factors have a significant impact on everyday operative know-how:

   - employees´ capacity to memorize important facts
   - the amount of know-how possessed
   - the ability to take notes efficiently
   - fast information management with digital reading techniques

   In addition, various types of thinking processes (linear, lateral, radiant) are going on at the same time at various levels of the organization.

2. **Relationship with information.** Which way does the employee think? How does his or her mind work? Is the employee left-brain dominant, i.e., thinking mostly with words, numbers, and logic? Are there so-called "artistic" employees whose world of thinking is based on right-brain skills, such as symbols, colorful images, and day dreaming?

3. **Forms of information.** The company can also be analyzed based on the appearance of information—the form in which the data is presented inside and outside the company. Main division into printed and electronic information can be used. Subdivisions include information units, classes, relationships, systems, and transfers. Figure 1.5 applies these three strategic areas to two hypothetical companies, A and B.

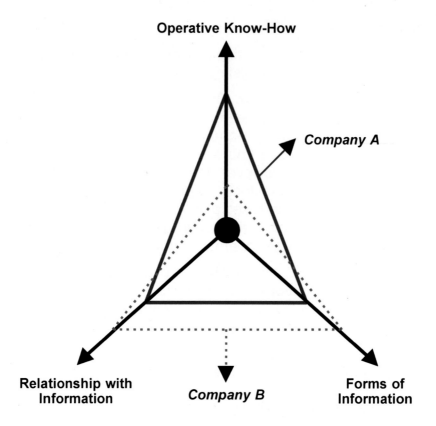

Figure 1.5: Companies A and B classified according to operative know-how, relationship with information, and forms of information.

A successful company will plan its strategy by taking into consideration the goals of both employees and the organization. These goals should be agreed upon jointly and their achievement should take place in an enjoyable and fun-filled environment, where the company emphasizes lifelong learning and training.

As mentioned earlier, a person with an academic degree has an average reading speed of 400 words per minute (wpm) just after graduation, but after a few years it drops to almost half that. The United Nations has reported the need to read at least 400 wpm in order to be "functionally and digitally literate" in today's society—to be able to cope with the increasing amount of information. This places many people at a great disadvantage in our society, where information is considered the fourth factor of production besides land, labor, and capital.

According to many forecasts, the amount of information available today will double every two to three years, with some sectors seeing this increase in only 12 to 15 months (see Figure 1.6, which shows one forecast). The trend is that this time span will progressively and continually shorten. Even if we are able to cope with this deluge of information at present, the likelihood is that very shortly we will be overwhelmed by it. As David Shenk in his book *Data Smog: Surviving the Information Glut* (1997) so appropriately put it: "Virtually anyone can very easily become an information glutton. We now face the prospect of information obesity. The more information thrown at us, the less we know; we are on the verge of culturally induced attention deficit disorder."

The importance of constantly practicing reading can never be emphasized enough. The more you practice your reading skills, the more your speed and understanding will improve.

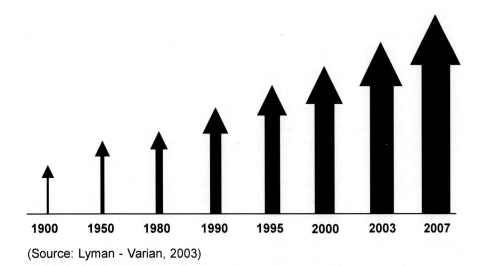

| 1900 | 1950 | 1980 | 1990 | 1995 | 2000 | 2003 | 2007 |

(Source: Lyman - Varian, 2003)

Figure 1.6: Forecast of the amount of all information available by the year 2007 (the size of the arrow indicates the accumulated volume of information available up to certain time periods).

Reading Exercises

All seven reading exercises can be done either from the book or directly from your computer screen at www.hrdpress.com/effective screenreading/exercises.html.

For all reading exercises, you should follow these guidelines:

1. Read for exactly 1 minute (60 seconds).

2. Have a timer that will automatically sound after 1 minute (or have a friend keep time). Make sure you don't have to glance at the clock.

3. Start the timer and begin to read for 1 minute.

4. When you hear the alarm, circle or underline the last word you read. If you read from the screen, set the pointer of the mouse or double-click the last word.

5. Calculate the amount of words you have read in 1 minute (wpm) and write it on the line after the text or on a piece of paper. In each exercise, there are dots in the left margin. The first dot indicates that somewhere on that line is the 100th word. The next dot indicates 200 words, etc. Each line has an average of 6 words. If you read 8 lines over the 100 mark, your total would be 100 + (8 x 6) = 148 words per minute. If you read so fast that you finish the text in under 1 minute, *start from the beginning again* and calculate the number of words accordingly. When calculating your wpm, all types of words are taken into consideration including even the shortest articles and prepositions. Hyphenated words are considered one word.

6. Transfer your results to the reading progression chart in Figure 2.23 at the end of Chapter 2. Indicate your speed in the column for each exercise by drawing a bar from 100 up to the number of words per minute you were able to read. Additionally, you can write the exact number on top of the bar.

Reading Exercise 0: Set the reference point. Read at normal speed and at normal level of comprehension. Read the following text or go to the Web page (www.hrdpress.com/effectivescreen reading/exercises.html). The purpose of the first exercise (Exercise 0) is to set your reference point—to see what is your current reading speed and level of understanding. Read the text at *normal speed* and at *normal level of comprehension.* In Chapter 2, you will find various techniques to improve your reading. This enables you to follow and monitor your progress all the time. Read the text for 1 minute and calculate the number of words based on the 100-word dots in the left margin.

Exercise 0: Behavior

Behavior can be described as the way in which all organisms, not just humans, act in response to various stimuli. This could be anything from turning on a heater when it becomes cold, to biting ones' nails when one becomes nervous. The stimulus is the event, which causes a certain response, the behavior. In the above examples, the stimuli are the temperature decreasing, and becoming nervous. It is not only humans who show behavior. All animals, even the smallest ones, exhibit behavior. It is believed that organisms are pre-programmed, before birth, with the ability to behave in certain ways. This kind of behavior is known as innate behavior. Innate behavior is behavior which is unlearned. It is also known as inbuilt, inborn and inherited behavior. Often, innate behavior is very important to enable organisms to survive in the early stages of life.

Learning occurs when existing behavior becomes modified as a result of experience. It relies on memory. This is because in order to change their behavior, an organism must remember what had happened previously when placed in the same situation. Habituation is a process of learning not to respond to stimuli that are not relevant to an organism's survival. For example, people living for a long time on a busy road begin to not notice the sound of heavy traffic driving past. Habituation is one of the simplest forms of learning. Although it is considered a form of learning, habituation does not actually really involve learning. It does however rely on memory.

There are many different learning types, each of which are defined by their experiences. *Imprinting* only occurs at a particular time in the early development of organisms. The chickens become imprinted to the first moving thing they see within the first 36 hours of their life. Newly hatched chickens form a strong and irrevocable bond with that first moving thing they see. Those first 36 hours are known as the critical period. Studies have been undertaken to show that if the mother is replaced with a moving rock or even a human, the chickens can be led to believe that the human or the rock is its mother.

Learning occurs when existing behavior becomes modified as a result of experience. It relies on memory. This is because in order to change their behavior, an organism must remember what had happened previously when placed in the same situation. Habituation is a process of learning not to respond to stimuli that are not relevant to an organism's survival. For example, people living for a long time on a busy road begin to not notice the sound of heavy traffic driving past. Habituation is one of the simplest forms of learning. Although it is considered a form of learning, habituation does not actually really involve learning. It does however rely on memory.

Imitation is a very simple form of learning. The organism involved simply copies an observed behavior. A good example of this is birds learning how to sing by imitating the sounds made by their parents.

● *Associative learning* occurs when an organism's response has been transferred from one stimulus to another. Associative learning is also known as conditioning. A very famous example of conditioning is Pavlov's dog. Pavlov, a Russian scientist discovered that each time he gave his dog meat powder, the dog would salivate. At the same time as giving the meat powder, Pavlov would ring a bell. Eventually, the dog would salivate whenever he heard the bell, even if it hadn't received any meat powder. Trial and error involves learning from your mistakes. Your behavior

● becomes more refined each time in order to increase your success in obtaining the most favorable outcome. Trial and error is used when learning to walk or ride a bike. Problem Solving is very complex learning. It is usually only observed in higher animals, i.e., humans and other primates such as apes and monkeys. People using problem solving visualize the situation and then think about the solutions. Although this process does involve some trial and error, success occurs more readily.

- *Associative learning* occurs when an organism's response has been transferred from one stimulus to another. Associative learning is also known as conditioning. A very famous example of conditioning is Pavlov's dog. Pavlov, a Russian scientist discovered that each time he gave his dog meat powder, the dog would salivate. At the same time as giving the meat powder, Pavlov would ring a bell. Eventually, the dog would salivate whenever he heard the bell, even if it hadn't received any meat powder. Trial and error involves learning from your mistakes. Your behavior be-

- comes more refined each time in order to increase your success in obtaining the most favorable outcome. Trial and error is used when learning to walk or ride a bike. Problem Solving is very complex learning. It is usually only observed in higher animals, i.e., humans and other primates such as apes and monkeys. People using problem solving visualize the situation and then think about the solutions. Although this process does involve some trial and error, success occurs more readily.

There is a wide range of behavior types: some that involve social interactions and some that are more individual. Maintenance Behavior, as it suggests, maintains an organism's well-being. Examples of maintenance behavior include eating, drinking and sleeping. Grooming, another form of maintenance behavior helps keep animals clean and free from germs. Many animals mark out and guard their own territory. This has many advantages including the exclusive use of the area's resources, such as food, water and shelter, by the area's inhabitants. Other animals of the same species are able to recognize territorial messages and generally don't enter an area marked as someone else's territory.

Reproductive behavior is very complex and involved many stages, including courtship, copulation and parenting. The readiness for mating is under hormonal control, which is largely under the control of environmental factors. Courtship rituals ensure that males and females of the same species are ready for mating at the same time and that they are in the same area when they are ready for mating. Communication indicating readiness to mate involves sound, physical appearance, touch and chemicals. Fertile females (animals) produce pheromones (chemicals) which stimulate the male's sense of smell. These chemicals indicate a readiness to mate. Colour and "dance" rituals are also used. (© bbc.co.uk)

Total number of words in 1 minute:_____

Please enter your result in the reading progression chart in Figure 2.23 at the end of Chapter 2 and subjectively estimate your understanding (Very well, Well, Sufficiently, or Little).

Summary and Onward

You have now learned about digital reading and a technique called SuperBrowse. You can use it with any book or computer manual when short of time. In addition, the concept of the learning organization was presented. In the next chapter, you will be introduced to specific techniques to dramatically increase your reading speed from the computer screen.

— 2 —
DIRECT Program—
Techniques for Effective
Screen Reading

DIRECT Program (DI = Digital, RE = Reading, C = Competency, T = Techniques) includes six different digital reading techniques to speed up your screen reading ability. We have carefully selected these six techniques from among various speed reading techniques since these give the best results for a computer screen. Using them properly will guarantee improved efficiency when reading text on screen. To start with, the TripleSpeed technique and the Computer Screen guide are demonstrated. You will learn to take optimal advantage of the eye-brain combination. The importance of working position, distance to the screen, and mental strength is explained as well as how to change previously learned habits. Our final technique will make you change gears and start reading with turbo speed. At the very end of the chapter, we will reveal what is the real benefit of DIRECT Program to you.

In today's society, we are all being offered access to the information superhighway—the Internet. Using traditional techniques when reading will no longer serve us. Just reading the text is not sufficient; we are expected to manage the total content—to absorb, comprehend, memorize, recall, and make a presentation of the information when necessary. These requirements are even further emphasized with the growing amount of new information on the Web.

Most people have their own beliefs and habits related to correct reading techniques and speeds. However, the necessity to evaluate habits will undoubtedly become stronger when new scientifically and empirically tested information on reading efficiency is released. Consequently, it is easier to adopt new, improved methods for everyday reading with the following factors in place:

- Updated information on how human eyes and the brain function

- Willingness, motivation, and need to change

- The persistence to cultivate the new habit—to practice it systematically

It is quite common for people to think that beliefs and practices are set in stone and cannot be varied or questioned. Listed below are some of these beliefs. Do you recognize some and can you relate to any of them?

1. You should not sub-vocalize (say words under your breath) because it slows down your speed when reading from the screen.

2. Pointing at the text on the monitor with any type of guide is wrong.

3. To appreciate the text and fully understand its contents you must read it slowly and carefully.

4. Start reading the book or the text on the screen from the very beginning and proceed to the end in order.

5. If you don't understand something, go back and clarify it for yourself before reading further.

6. You need to use mainly the left side of your brain when reading.

7. Each word on the computer screen must be read separately.

8. If you encounter a word that you don't understand, look it up immediately from your electronic dictionary or other reference material.

9. Reading faster will result in poor understanding and a subsequent drop in comprehension.

10. Motivation has minor importance in reading speed.

11. To rest or exercise your eyes regularly is not necessary.

12. You should understand 100 percent of the text.

13. Peripheral vision is about the page width.

14. You can only read the information that is in your direct visual focus.

15. Don't pause until you have finished reading all the text.

As you learn the main digital reading techniques and do the exercises that follow, you will gradually find out if the points mentioned are true or not.

3S Technique: Use the TripleSpeed Technique

If you are in a relaxed mood and there is no urgency to do anything or go anywhere, like walking on a beach, you walk slowly forward. This is because there is no pressure on you to do otherwise. On the other hand, if you need to escape something or have to catch a bus—you have some kind of objective in mind—you run with determination. Reading can be compared to this. By taking advantage of the eye-brain system, you can select the speed and "walk fast" through the text to reach your goal efficiently. If not pressed with deadlines or any other objectives, you can "walk slowly" through the text and relax yourself with the words and their meaning.

A technique that will easily double your reading speed with minimum practice is called the *TripleSpeed technique (3S)*. The 3S technique will ensure the productive use of eyes, since it is based on the knowledge of actual eye movement. It is imperative to know how the eyes move during the screen reading process and why you need to exercise them in the right way.

Your Magnificent Eyes

The eye is more than just an organ for vision. The cooperation between the eyes and the brain constitutes the basis for abstract and intelligent thinking. For most people, over 90 percent of new information obtained comes through the sense of vision. With one glance, we are "flooded" with about 1.5 million sight stimuli. The eye can actually be considered an "intelligence robot" developed during human evolution. It can sort out the most important information from the field of view and send it to be processed by the brain. An American psychologist, Dr. Renskin, has developed a slide test that illustrates the eye-brain cooperation. Two almost identical slides are changed back and forth. In between, a so-called misleading flicker-picture is being flashed. The result is that the spectator thinks he sees the same picture over and over again—the eye does not consider it necessary to convey the changes further.

The ability to see is an extremely intricate and complex physical activity that may be susceptible to various outside influences. These could potentially affect sight, such as:

- Eyeballs need to be moved in a coordinated way.

- Eyeballs need to be able to track a moving object while you are moving yourself.

- Eyelids blink once a second, faster when nervous.

- Eyes function smoothly only if enough liquid is produced by the tear glands. Tears are produced by emotions or other visual, auditory, or kinesthetic stimuli.

- The direction and focus of the eyes change on average three to four times per second.

The principles of the 3S technique can easily be realized by carrying out a simple exercise.

Ask your friend/partner to read from a monitor of a computer for a few minutes in such a way that you can observe his/her eyes. Notice the eyes during reading and try to sketch the movement you see on paper.

Did you notice the following things happen when your friend/partner was reading:

1. **The eyes made several brief stops while reading the text.** The stopping points—actually short pauses—are called *fixations*. To "see clearly," the eyes *must* stop on words that you read. It is natural to fixate on certain information in order to understand it and form a clear picture in the brain. After stopping, the eyes continue to the next set of information.

2. **Sometimes the eyes seemed to go back over the text.** It is as though the eyes were checking that the word read was also understood and no information was missed. The reader cannot rely on his understanding of the text and, just to be sure, *re*reads those words again. This is called *back-skipping*—returning almost as a habit to those immediate words just read. Back-skipping is only slightly different from *regression*—consciously returning back to words that the reader feels have been missed or misunderstood. Both back-skipping and regression are among the biggest time wasters in screen reading and can decrease your speed by as much as 50 percent. Primary reasons for regression are poor vocabulary and lack of confidence in the eye/brain power. Restricted vocabulary is definitely a substantial pitfall, because it is impossible to comprehend the meaning of a sentence, especially the key concepts, if you don't know the meaning of various words.

3. **There was a considerable amount of time wasted searching for the start of the next line.** A problem related to regression worth mentioning is slow *recovery time*. Like back-skipping and regression, most people are totally unaware of this deficiency. Recovery time is the time it takes your eyes to move from the end of one line to the beginning of the next. High-speed cameras, which are capable of registering the movement of eyes with the accuracy of 1/1,000 of a second, can easily detect that an untrained reader spends as much as one-third (33 percent) of his time searching for the next line on the screen. As no information comes into the brain, slow recovery time is definitely a big time consumer.

4. **Sometimes the eyes wandered off the monitor.** This can easily happen as a result of some outside disturbance or internal boredom. Getting back to the screen and especially to the correct line can take some time. Studies conducted at the Finnish Institute of Occupational Health demonstrate that the eyes can wander off the monitor up to 18 times in a minute while reading. Most often this is a result of poor concentration. People are "reading" in one place, while their mind is somewhere else.

5. **The eyes stopped at least four to five times on one line.** The number of fixations per line can vary greatly depending on the reader. Did you count how many times your friend stopped per line before moving on to the next one? If you were able to take a group of three or four words at a time instead of one or two, you could easily double or triple your reading speed.

6. **It was possible to hear the voice of the reader at times.** *Vocalization*—reading the text aloud—severely limits your capacity. You just cannot read and comprehend much faster than you talk. The average top speed for human speech is around 300 words per minute. Thus vocalization should be reduced to a minimum; preferably one should not do it at all. On the other hand, *subvocalization*—pronouncing the words in your head (in the mind) while reading—cannot, and actually should not, be eliminated totally, because it is a natural part of the reading process. There is always a slight movement in the larynx due to the phonetic method taught at school. You should therefore stop using vocalization and become more selective with subvocalization in order to take advantage of this natural, universal habit as an aid to memory. You can pick up the key words from the text and "shout" them internally. In this way, the important information stands out from the rest and is attached to your auditory memory in a much stronger way.

Figure 2.1 shows how fixations, regression/back-skipping, and wanderings take place when the lines of text are read.

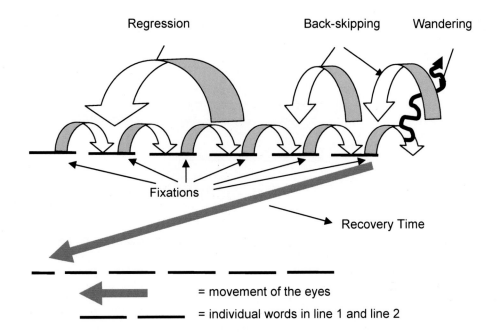

Figure 2.1: Fixations, regression/back-skipping, recovery time, and wandering in reading.

The Three Elements of the 3S Technique

The 3S technique consists of three partially overlapping parts (see Figure 2.2). These are fixation, moving forward, and concentration. Learn and apply the 3S technique to your everyday reading and you will drastically improve your reading speed on the computer screen.

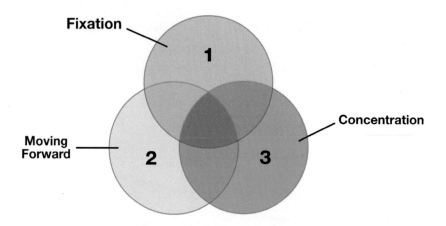

Figure 2.2: The three overlapping parts of the 3S Technique: fixation, moving forward, and concentration.

1. **Shorten the fixation time and take more words at each stop.** The time needed for one fixation (stopping the eyes on the word[s]) by a non-trained reader varies between ¼ and 1½ seconds, mainly depending on the length and the complexity of the word. However, there is no need to rest on these words for such a long time, because the eyes have an unbelievable capability to grasp information in just a fraction of a second. Therefore, try to shorten the fixation time and drop it down to ¼ to ½ of a second even with longer words. Pick out the key words (substantives, verbs, names, numbers) and skim over the joining ones (articles, prepositions, adverbs). The eye muscles tire very quickly if they have to refocus on every word. Consequently, try to expand your vision to grasp more words with each fixation. Instead of taking only one word, try to take two. Of course it is easier to take shorter words at a time. Instead of letting your eyes stop on only two words at a time, try to take in short phrases. The eyes are capable of seeing many words in focused vision, as we will explain later. The maximum measured capacity for human eyes confirms that they can take in up to five bits of information (equivalent to five words) in 1/100 of a second. A quick calculation reveals that the maximum reading speed could rise as high as 30,000 wpm if it only depended on the capacity of the eyes. Whether the brain is capable of processing such a large

amount of text in a 1-minute time frame and if the reader can maintain concentration on the topic are, of course, different questions.

2. **Move forward only.** Condition yourself to only move forward—you will no longer back-skip or regress. Generally speaking, to comprehend the main idea of the text, it is only necessary to understand 50 to 70 percent of its contents, while invariably the amount of key words in a text is somewhere around 5 to 20 percent of its total. This means that only every fifth or less than tenth word has real relevance to the reader. Consequently, there is no need to understand every word. Be confident that a word or part of a text not understood exactly at a certain moment will be explained later in other words and expressions. Most writers use this repetition to emphasize their key messages.

3. **Concentrate on the screen.** A speed *fast enough* will prevent the brain from getting bored. As the brain works with associations, your interpretation of a word may not be the same as the author's. With an increase in reading speed, you are less likely to stray from the author's intent because you do not give the brain time to make unnecessary associations. When high levels of interest are maintained, wandering is minimized and you tend to stay focused on the screen. If your reading mood is distracted because you are nervous, stressed, tired, or your interest and attitude toward the subject is low, your reading speed will definitely suffer. At these negative states of mind, it is advisable to do something else for a short period of time and then try again.

Reading Exercise 1: Use 3S. Read the following text or go to the Web page (www.hrdpress.com/effectivescreenreading/exercises. html). The objective of Reading Exercise 1 is to use the 3S technique learned in this chapter. Read the text for 1 minute and calculate the number of words based on the 100-word dots in the left margin. Concentrate on the page, keep moving forward only, take as many words as possible at each stop, and make the fixation time very short.

Reading Exercise 1: Smoke Ban Proposal

The government would be guilty of double standards if it did not enforce a full ban on smoking in public places, the British Medical Association says. As consultation on a partial ban ends, ministers are launching a campaign warning of second-hand smoke dangers. The BMA said the campaign smacked of double standards if the government didn't change its plans, which would still allow smoking in food-free pubs.

Health officials said it worked alongside other government actions. The Royal College of Nursing has already joined calls for a tougher smoking ban than the one proposed, which would exempt private members' clubs and pubs not serving food. Public Health Minister Caroline Flint said the government's £5m television and radio advertising campaign was designed to show people that they were often most at risk of the dangers of smoking in the places they felt safest. "It is clear that both smokers and non-smokers don't appreciate the full dangers of second-hand smoke," she said.

The TV adverts—to coincide with the end of the public consultation period on the proposed ban—show a group of family and friends relaxing at home watching TV where one person is smoking. If the government is aware of the hazards, how can it defend only a partial ban on smoking in public places? As the advert progresses the smoke moves around the group, snaking around their necks and revealing the long-term damage it can cause.

The government has also released the findings of a survey of more than 1,000 adults, which found 60% of smokers do not ask for permission to smoke, while a fifth of non-smokers do not feel comfortable asking someone not to light-up near them. Dr Vivienne Nathanson, head of science and ethics at the BMA, said: "If the government is aware of the hazards, how can it defend only a partial ban on smoking in public places?" The advert comes as research suggests many pubs will stop serving food to escape the ban. The survey, by Cancer Research UK and Action on Smoking and Health, indicates that the number of exempt pubs could rise to 40% from 29% which would currently qualify. In some of the most deprived areas, it could be as high as 50%, the survey warns.

Research published in the British Medical Journal has shown that second-hand smoke kills 11,000 people in the UK each year—the equivalent of about 30 a day. There is no hard evidence that second-hand smoke kills. But Simon Clark, director of smokers' lobby group Forest said smokers were developing "warning fatigue." I think people switch off to these campaigns; there is just too much anti-smoking sentiment out there."

The government has said it has received thousands of responses to its proposals since launching its consultation in June. BBC health correspondent Jane Dreaper says that as the consultation period ends, lobby groups on both sides of the smoking argument
● are firing their final shots in what has become a fierce public relations battle. Members of Cancer Research UK will present a petition at Downing Street later, while the smokers' lobby group Forest has placed advertisements in national newspapers.

The Royal College of Nursing, along with more than 5,000 nurses and supporters, has written to the Department of Health demanding a full ban. Under the plans all enclosed public places and workplaces would be smoke free, unless specifically exempted, by 2008. This would cover hospitals, schools, rail stations, shops, restaurants plus pubs where food is prepared and served. Dr. Charmain Griffiths, spokesperson for
● the British Heart Foundation, said: "The government still has the chance to choose the only sensible and workable solution: a full smoking ban in all enclosed public places, including all pubs." (©bbc.co.uk)

Total number words in 1 minute: _____

Please enter your result in the reading progression chart in Figure 2.23 at the end of Chapter 2, and subjectively estimate your understanding (Very well, Well, Sufficiently, or Little).

Computer Screen (CS) Guide Technique: Use a Guide

When looking for a piece of information or a number in the phone book, people unconsciously try to speed up the search by assisting their eyes with a finger. The same thing happens occasionally when trying to find a word in a dictionary. What is the reason for using the finger? The answer is obvious: To find the required information *faster*. However, when reading a book or a computer screen, the eyes freely wander among the text without any physical assistance.

Small children, especially during their early stages of learning and reading at school, automatically use their finger(s) to guide their eyes word by word. In the beginning, they read syllable-by-syllable and then word-by-word gradually speeding up. If they continue to use their finger as a pointer in the upper classes, teachers will sooner or later ask them to stop doing so, as in their opinion this slows down the reading. Probably teachers have never thought that the child could move his finger faster on the text! How fast can you actually move your fingers on a page? Are there limits? On the other hand, is assistance with a finger or the use of some other kind of pointer—a guide—useful at all?

To illustrate this, take the following short test with a friend.

Exercise: Guiding the Eyes

1. Ask your friend to trace (moving only his or her eyes) the outside of an imaginary circle (approximately 3 feet wide) hanging in the air.

2. Observe the eyes and draw the "circle" on a piece of paper.

3. Now, use your finger to trace the same sized circle in front of your friend's eyes. Ask him or her to follow the movement of your finger with his or her eyes (not moving his or her head) and again, draw the circle on another piece of paper.

4. Compare the two circles. Which one resembles a true circle more and why?

Close to 100 percent find that the second circle (the guided one) resembles a true and more accurate circle than the first one. Experiments show that the eyes work more efficiently and locate the required information faster if they are being led and pulled along by some type of guide.

Using a Computer Screen Guide

A guide recommended for computer displays is an extendible, thin telescopic-type pointer, the length of which is adjustable. It is called a computer screen guide (or CS guide). Other types of CS guides include chopsticks, knitting needles, or the antenna from your portable radio. Make sure your guide has a rounded, plastic head or you may scratch your screen. To avoid this problem, it is advisable to use a laser-pointer, moving the beam on the display. Whatever method you adopt is really not that important. What *is* important is that you do adopt one.

Advantages to using a CS guide:

1. Both back-skipping and regression are eliminated, as the guide forces your eyes to *go forward only*.

2. Your comprehension and concentration will be improved, as the movement of the guide *keeps you on the page*.

3. Because the human eyes are designed to follow movement (survival aspect) and are more comfortable doing so, using a guide will *relax the eyes*. This will result in increased reading speed and the eyes will be less tired.

4. The guide offers a definitive helping tool for a quick and smooth transition *from one line to another*, saving lost recovery time. The time to find the starting point of the next line will be reduced to around 5 percent of the total reading time, instead of the typical 20 to 30 percent without a guide.

When using a CS guide, follow these rules:

1. Move the guide smoothly from left to right only. Consequently, the guide will automatically eliminate back-skipping, because the eyes are bound to follow the guide.

2. Keep the guide relaxed in your right or left hand. Glide it on top or under the text line. Move the guide from the beginning until the end of the line. Move it again to the beginning of the next line and continue. Pull your eyes along. When you notice improvement and the technique feels comfortable, skip the beginnings and endings of each line only taking the middle part. Practice and shorten the line until it is enough to move the guide in a wavy line down the middle of the page. The arrows in the figures below show how the eyes follow the guide when moving along the lines with different techniques.

Figures 2.3 through 2.9 illustrate the different techniques you can use with a CS guide.

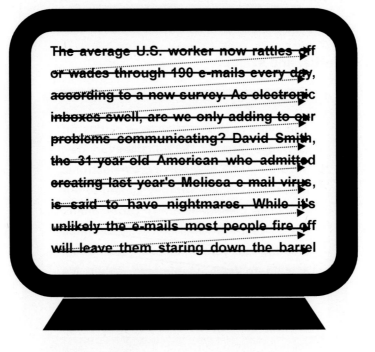

Figure 2.3: Whole line sweep.

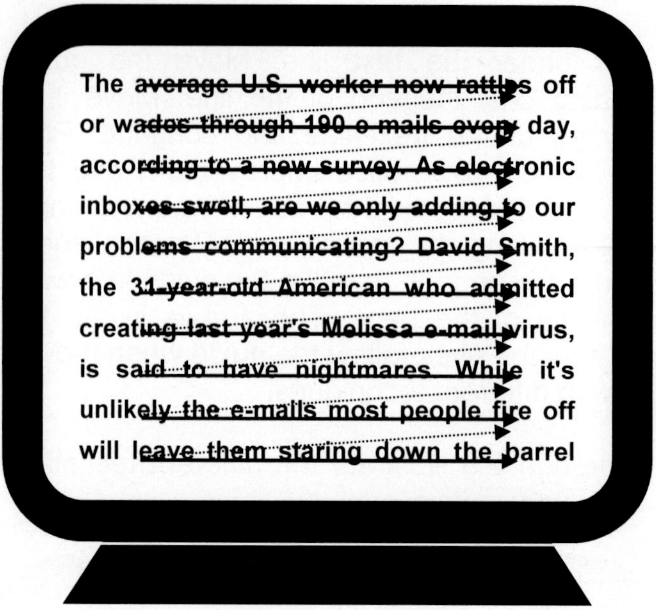

Figure 2.4: Partial line sweep.

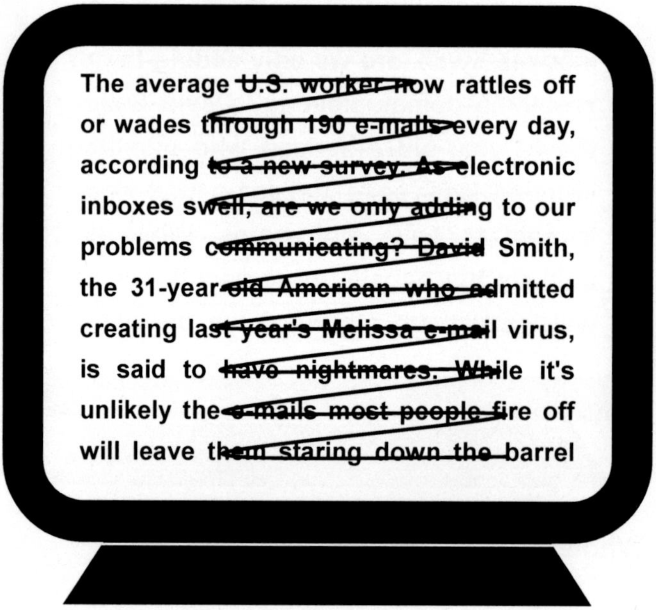

Figure 2.5: Zipper.

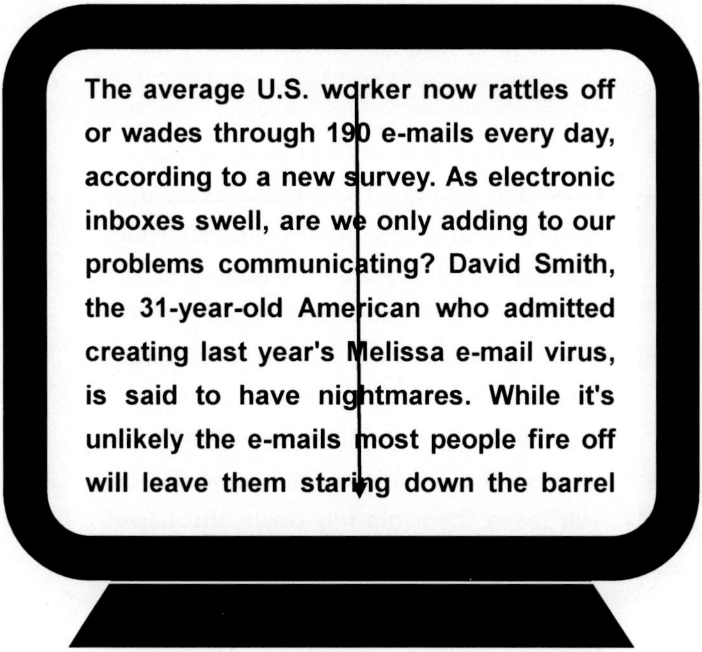

Figure 2.6: Vertical sweep.

When you practice and become more skillful in using a guide, you may want to try more advanced guiding techniques, for example:

- The double-guide—using the guide and the mouse arrow together
- The "S"—reading multiple lines at the same time
- The "Skimming S"—skimming rapidly through (Web) pages for an overall view

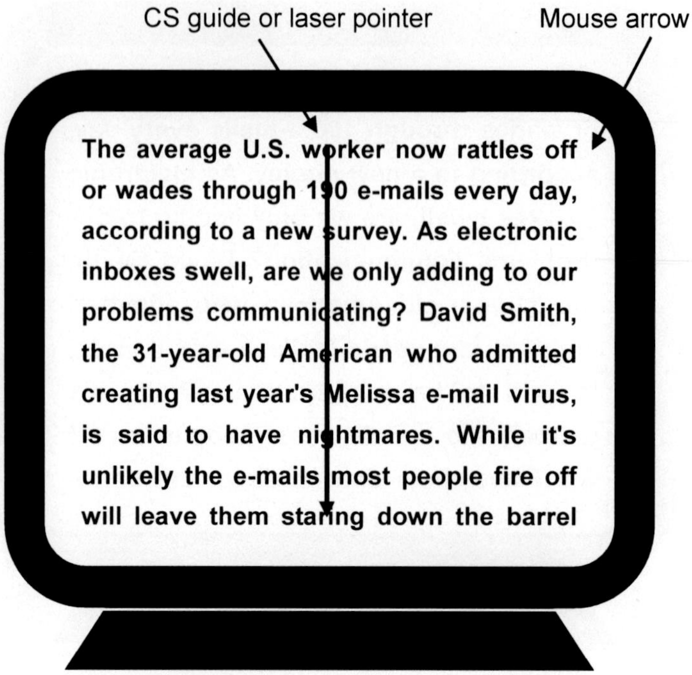

CS guide or laser pointer · Mouse arrow

> The average U.S. worker now rattles off or wades through 190 e-mails every day, according to a new survey. As electronic inboxes swell, are we only adding to our problems communicating? David Smith, the 31-year-old American who admitted creating last year's Melissa e-mail virus, is said to have nightmares. While it's unlikely the e-mails most people fire off will leave them staring down the barrel

Figure 2.7: Double-guide.

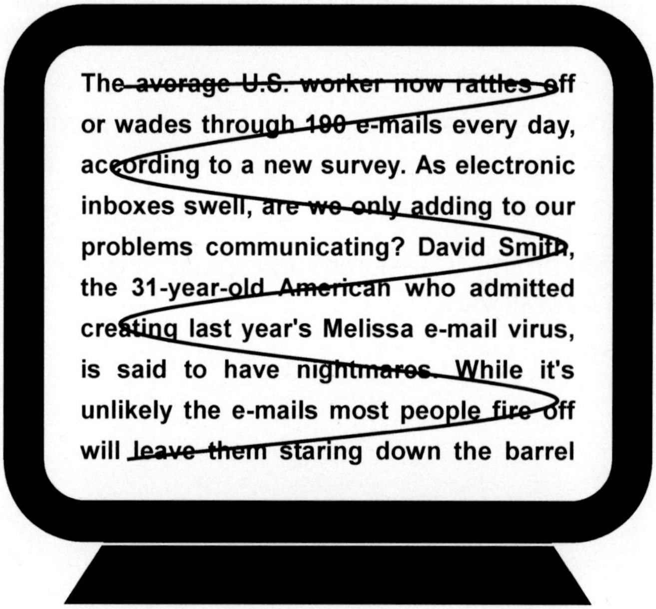

> The average U.S. worker now rattles off or wades through 190 e-mails every day, according to a new survey. As electronic inboxes swell, are we only adding to our problems communicating? David Smith, the 31-year-old American who admitted creating last year's Melissa e-mail virus, is said to have nightmares. While it's unlikely the e-mails most people fire off will leave them staring down the barrel

Figure 2.8: "S."

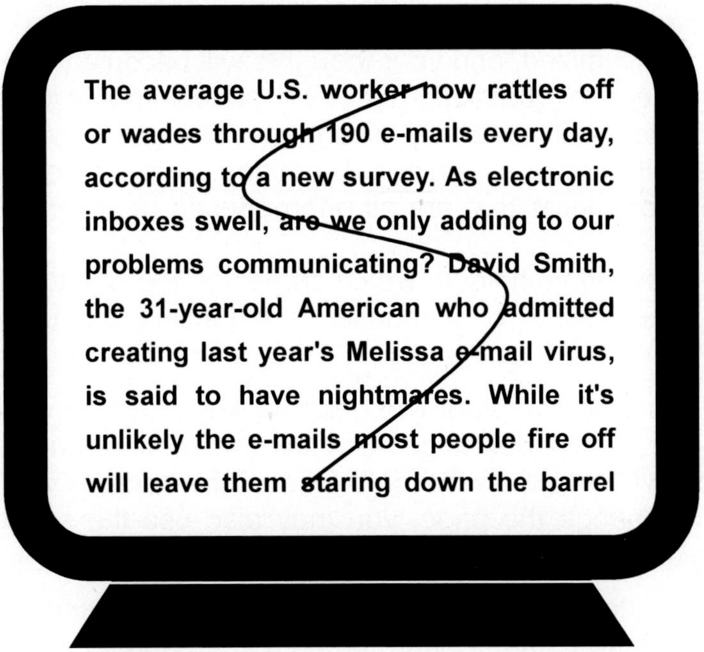

Figure 2.9: "Skimming S."

Guiding Improves Ergonomy

Reading efficiency depends greatly on the size, quality, and flickering of the screen as well as on the amount and layout of the information presented. The text often *flickers* without the viewer noticing it. As various factors influence flickering, we have devoted a section in Chapter 3 to discuss this issue.

The tool used for guiding the eyes must be adaptable to all types of situations. For example, your physical distance to the screen may vary during a working day, depending on your mood and office placement. The recommended viewing distance to the display of 2 to 3 feet can sometimes temporarily become under 20 inches and sometimes extend to more than a yard. The guide should be adaptable to all these situations.

By using a guide, you will gain some additional benefits related to an improved ergonomic working environment. Your reading will become more efficient, as you may position yourself a little bit further away from the screen. This allows you to grasp more information with each natural fixation. The amount of work done by the eyes is minimized, and your thoughts will become more focused on the subject in question. Eyestrain so commonly experienced with computers will gradually disappear. The guide will also help eliminate stiff necks, restricted breathing, and sometimes even lower back problems that are all often caused by incorrect seating positions.

The following technique, which combines the CS guide and the use of a line spacer or a mouse, is especially useful with Web pages:

1. Press the computer line pacer (↓ key on the keyboard) with your right index finger or click the mouse pointing at the "down"-arrow on the right side of the screen (vertical bar). To change the page, you may also use the space bar for more rapid movement.

2. Hold the CS guide relaxed in your left hand. Adjust its length to be appropriate to the screen and let your arm lean in to your body. A laser pointer will do the job just as well.

3. Reveal the lines one at a time using the line pacer (or the mouse or the space bar). Stop the movement of the page to let your eyes fixate on the text.

4. Let the CS guide (or the beam of the laser pen) cruise forward as the pages reveal themselves to you. Use the appropriate guiding technique depending on the purpose of your reading.

As you pick up speed, you can switch from the line pacer to the "page down" key. This will force your eyes to skim or scan entire pages of type in one swoop.

Relaxation and Concentration

The long-lasting basis for faster reading with excellent comprehension is achieved through high concentration. The most efficient way to accomplish a high level of concentration is to relax the mind and the body.

During relaxation, the brain waves, which measure the working frequency of the brain, change from beta (β) to alpha (α). Typically alpha frequency varies between 9 to 13 Hz and beta frequency from 14 to 30 Hz. The lower the frequency, the more relaxed you feel yourself and the more receptive you are to absorbing new information. Figure 2.10 illustrates human brain waves and their frequencies.

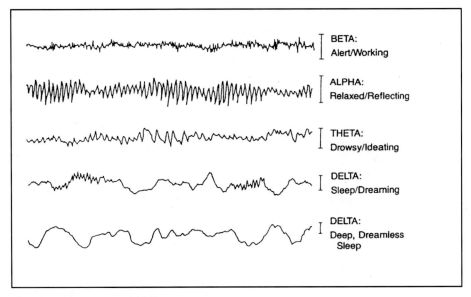

(Source: Herrmann, 1996)

Figure 2.10: Human brain waves (frequencies).

We will present five simple relaxation exercises in this chapter. The maximum time for each is 1 minute. They can all be done at your workstation without anyone noticing what you are actually doing. Consequently, these exercises have three advantages: speed, privacy, and most importantly, they can be carried out at your workstation. The topic of concentration will be dealt with more thoroughly in Chapter 3.

Relaxation Exercise A: 4 x 4 Breathing

1. Start by exhaling slowly and count to 4 in your mind.

2. Count again to 4 before starting to inhale.

3. Slowly inhale by counting to 4.

4. Count to 4 before starting to exhale.

5. Repeat for 1 minute.

Repeat the cycle at least four times. If you feel dizzy or uncomfortable, stop the exercise and try again later.

Reading Exercise 2: Use CS Guide. Read the following text or go to Web page (www.hrdpress.com/effectivescreenreading/exercises. html). Make sure that you use a guide (e.g., telescopic pointer, mouse cursor, laser pointer) and the 3S technique learned in this chapter. Read the text for 1 minute and calculate the number of words based on the 100-word dots in the left margin.

Reading Exercise 2: Advances in Technology

About forty years ago, only the government could afford a computer. At this time computers required large rooms for storage and teams of highly trained computer people to operate them. Things have changed since then. Computers now come in all different shapes and sizes—from systems large as a room to tiny notepad computers. Computers also fit all different lifestyles and budgets, costing millions of dollars for large company installations to the hundreds of dollars for personal home computers that students and families can use. Anyone can use a computer, it doesn't matter if you are a specialist computer operator to a teenager using the word processor for school assignments. Computer systems have become easier to operate over the years, Fifteen years ago complex commands were required to perform simple tasks such as copying files. Today, these operations can be done with a few clicks of the mouse. Most personal computer systems are designed so that everyone is able to use the system to store, calculate and work in an organized and efficient manner.

A computer is a machine that contains millions of tiny electronic circuits. These circuits are arranged so that the computer can use them to perform mathematical calculations, understand logical conditions, store and retrieve numbers from its memory and sort information. Whether a computer is used to control a traffic light or store a school assignment, the computer performs one of these tasks. Of course, expensive company and government computers are larger and faster than an average home computer. To be able to predict changing weather patterns for example, the Government must store and process great volumes of information. Similar organizations like NASA who need large amounts of processing, use mainframe computers to handle the immense load. Mainframe computers can store huge amounts of data in memory and can also process the data at extremely high speeds. They are built with many connections to other devices, which allow them to communicate with a number of other computers and computer-related devices.

Mainframes are the fastest, and most powerful computers. Obviously, they are also the most expensive. Mainframes can cost millions of dollars and must be stored in specially designed buildings. This is because these computer systems will generally be so large as to take up roomfuls of space. Many data processing specialists are needed to program these computers. Many companies that have
● complicated tasks will use much smaller but very powerful computers called workstations. Workstations are smaller and cheaper than mainframes, so they do not require special facilities. Yet, they may require a computer specialist to operate them.

However, most computer users (like you and me), use microcomputers to handle small jobs such as word processing and personal accounting. Micros are much smaller and cheaper than both mainframes and workstations. Their essential circuitry—known as the central processing unit—can be found on a single tiny silicon chip. This type of chip is called a microprocessor. Micro
● computers are seen in everyday life, including the Macintosh and the PC. Your PC at home, school, or work is a microcomputer. The differences between mainframes and microcomputers become less as computer technology improves. Mainframes can process

more data, and process it faster. However, each new model of microcomputer is more powerful than the last. In the last few years, microcomputer memories have grown and the chips have become much faster. They have been designed to work with more computer-related devices, allowing them to handle more varied applications. As a result, applications that were handled by mainframes are now, in some instances, handled by workstations and microcomputers. You probably have seen this type of improvement in technology in the fact that your home computer now can be used as a video game machine, with the introduction of the latest video games on compact disk (CD).

So, computers come in different shapes and sizes, but they all work in the same way. Data travels through a computer's circuits in the form of electronic pulses. The route that the pulses take through the circuits depends on the type of instructions that the computer program gives. For example, when you are using a word processing program, the electronic pulses travel in a way which enables the words to be produced on the screen. This program transfers information by sending it through one or more possible routes of the circuits. Information such as words and numbers is stored using a binary coding. A binary coding is a numbering system based on the two values of 0 and 1. These are the only digits that computers understand. Words and numbers must be converted to a sequence of ones and zeros. This is because a computer signal is digital and a binary digital system can be on and off, just like a binary number can be 0 or 1.

When a computer receives a series of electronic pulses, it treats them like binary code. The 1s are parts of the series in which the electricity is on and the 0s are parts of the series where the electricity is off. It doesn't matter what the series of pulses are doing; if you are adding, storing information, or evaluating it, it is handled in binary code.
(©bbc.co.uk)

Total number of words in 1 minute:_____

Please enter your result in the reading progression chart in Figure 2.24 at the end of Chapter 2 and subjectively estimate your understanding (Very well, Well, Sufficiently, or Little).

Pyramidal Technique: Use Maximum Vision Capacity

During the past 20 years, there has been a notable increase in work-related health problems. A growing number of workers complain about headaches, injured wrists, sore necks, tight shoulder muscles, and pain in the back after a working day. This is especially true among employees working in offices. However, knowledge on how to improve working environment has increased along with the use of ergonomic studies. Consequently, *ergonomics* play a more and more important role when offices are designed and equipment is purchased.

One of the leading countries in research in this area is Finland. According to the studies done by the Finnish Institute of Work and Health, continuous neck and shoulder problems were close to 40 percent higher in 2006 than in 1998. This rise is global and can be attributed to three factors:

1. The growing number of computer terminals in the work-place

2. The increase in time spent reading information on the screen

3. The use of the keyboard and mouse with the increased use of e-mail and the Internet

In 1984, only 17 percent of employees in Finland were using computers on a daily basis, but this figure went up to 56 percent in 1996 and to 66 percent in 2003. Estimations for 2007 exceed 70 percent (Finnish Institute of Occupational Health, www.hl.fi).

One area of ergonomics studies the movement of the human eye on the computer screen. The vision capacity, and especially the eye, is extremely adaptive to various situations and lighting conditions. The text in books and other printed material is stationary, making it easy to fixate on a group of words and then continue. However, when reading from the computer screen, the eyes are facing a tremendous challenge. Depending on the quality of the screen, the eyes must compensate for different types of vibrations, not only from the screen itself, but also from the surrounding lighting. Reflections to and from the screen can greatly distract the reader and deteriorate comprehension (see Chapter 3).

The vision capacity can be trained to capture the electronic text faster and to grasp more information with each fixation. Two types of vision capacity can be distinguished: *peripheral* vision and *focused* vision.

Peripheral Vision

With a short exercise, it is possible to measure the scope of vision both horizontally and vertically. Do the following two exercises.

Keep the tips of your index fingers horizontally in front of you and level with your eyes. Now start wriggling the tips of your index fingers and slowly move them apart, continuing to wriggle. Keep your head still and your eyes focused straight ahead. See how far you can move your fingers apart before you no longer see movement. When this happens, measure (roughly) the distance. This is called the horizontal vision, as shown in Figure 2.11.

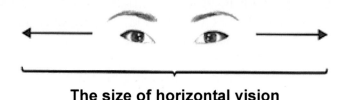

The size of horizontal vision

Figure 2.11: Horizontal vision.

Do exactly the same thing with your fingertips, but this time put them vertically in front of your eyes and start pulling them apart. Measure the distance when you can no longer see movement out of the top and bottom of your field of vision. This distance is called the vertical vision, as shown in Figure 2.12.

The size of vertical vision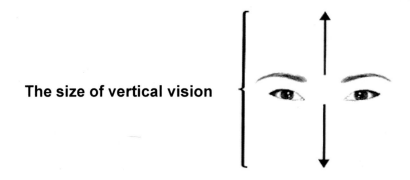

Figure 2.12: Vertical vision.

For many people, the horizontal vision is bigger than the length of their arms, in the range of 1 to 2 meters, perhaps even bigger. The vertical vision is smaller, being restricted by the eyebrow and cheekbone, but nonetheless it often comes close to one meter. Thus the peripheral vision (colloquially known as the landscape vision), which includes both the horizontal and vertical visions, can easily be in the range of 1 to 2 m² measured from only 20 cm from the eyes. In this area we can place four normal computer screens as a minimum!

A 15-inch screen is about 8½" x 11" in size and a 17-inch screen is about the size of a two-page spread in a book. An interesting question can be posed: Would it be possible with only one fixation to capture the contents of one whole line or even one whole paragraph on the screen? Do the eyes have the physical capacity for this? Well, at least the peripheral vision is not a limiting factor.

As explained earlier in the CS guide section, the eyes are designed to follow any type of movement within the field of vision. The human eye has 130 million vision cells—light receivers in each one. There are two types of vision cells, namely cones and rods, all of which are located in the back part of the eyeball—the retina. Over 80 percent are located in the peripheral vision and less than 20 percent have been devoted to the focused vision. Traditionally, people have been taught to concentrate on using this 20 percent of the visual capacity. However, the real computer speed reader will train him- or herself to utilize all of the untapped potential of over 260 million light receivers that are working and registering information all the time. As the landscape vision is "well equipped," you can occasionally perceive your friend's computer screen at the next workstation in this area of your sight. Consequently, the flickering from his or her screen can greatly influence your concentration and thus deteriorate your reading efficiency. If possible, eliminate this distraction by installing a screen or a lightweight movable wall.

Focused Vision—Group Words in a Pyramid Shape

It is not enough to "see" the whole screen. We must also focus on it, because we need to read the text and see pictures, graphics, symbols, links, etc. The area that your eyes clearly see and read is called the *focused vision*. The size of your focused vision will ultimately determine your true reading capacity.

You can measure the size of your focused vision with the following exercise.

Take a look at the sentence below and focus your eyes on the word *huge* under the arrow. Keep looking at this word and try to see how many words you can clearly distinguish and read from the right and how many from the left at the same time. Remember not to move your eyes from one side to the other.

"The capacity of the brain is so huge that we can never use it totally."

How many words did you see? Try now the same exercise, but move the text a little bit *farther away* from your eyes. Can you see more words?

The size of the focused vision is normally one or two words. With a little practice you can increase it up to three, four, or even five words. A well-trained computer speed reader can take a whole line with only one fixation.

You probably saw more words when you moved the text farther away from your eyes. The reason for this is that the text being farther away occupies less space in the focused vision. The area "reserved" for focused vision is located in the back of the eye-ball—in the retina—and is called the *fovea*. The size of the fovea represents only 0.1 percent of the visual field. This is the area in which all words read are seen clearly. Consequently, if text is moved farther away from the eyes, its relative size becomes smaller and therefore more words can be accommodated in the fovea at the same time.

Pyramidal Exercises

Your focused vision is like a muscle and needs training. You can only see the progress if you make this effort regularly. Figures 2.13 through 2.18 have exercises that will help you train and expand your focused vision.

The first exercises contain numbers. Try to read all the numbers on each line by focusing your eyes on the middle number (concentrate on the line drawn down the center of each row). Make an effort to see *clearly* all the numbers to the left and to the right without moving your eyes. Use your CS guide to assist in staying on the line.

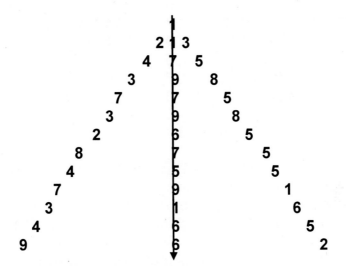

Figure 2.13: Pyramidal Exercise 1.

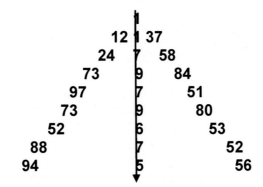

Figure 2.14: Pyramidal Exercise 2.

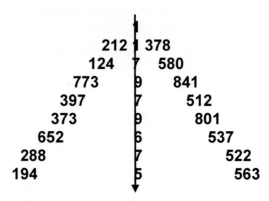

Figure 2.15: Pyramidal Exercise 3.

How many numbers in total were you able to see clearly to the right and to the left without moving your eyes?

Next you can try the same with text. Read the material formatted in a pyramidal shape and focus your eyes on the line drawn down the middle of the text. Again, concentrate and make a conscious effort to see clearly as many words or letters as possible to the right and to the left. Try not to move your eyes. Use a CS guide to assist in staying on the line.

In
the
last
ten years
there has been
an increase in neck,
shoulder, and back pain
problems among the office
workers. Many books have been
written on how to improve our ways
and habits of working, but still more and
more office people have severe headaches
sore wrists and necks, tight muscles, and pain in the
lower back area after the working days. At the same time,
we can notice a huge increase in the use of computers at the
offices and also in the time spent reading the information on the screen.

Figure 2.16: Pyramidal Exercise 4.

Imagine that you are "a screen reader athlete" in a fitness class. With this pyramidal training program, you can increase your reading muscle. The following exercises contain more pyramids of various sizes and should be completed in the same manner as Exercise 4.

In
this
little-known
university town at
the northern extreme
of the Gulf of Bothnia,
an army of Nordic computer
nerds looks poised to overrun
America's Internet innovators and
software supremos as the desktop-
dominated world goes wireless. Nowhere
has mobile communication caught on as it has
in sparsely populated Finland, where nearly 70 percent
of the 5.3 million residents are armed with wireless phones
and an ever-expanding array of tools, games, and services.

Mobile
communications
have changed the way
Finns work, play, and see
themselves in the world. This
modest country once better known
for global supremacy in suicides and
heavy drinking is taking the lead in developing
Internet-accessible handsets and services that will
let consumers carry the power of a personal computer
in their pockets. Although the phones can't do all that a
home PC can, Finnish companies have soared to the forefront
with services that allow users to check news, sports, and weather
wherever they are, as well as read their horoscopes or biorhythms,
order food, pay bills, buy Christmas presents, and collect e-mail.

Figure 2.17: Pyramidal Exercise 5.

(continued)

Only
about
25 percent
of U.S. citizens
own mobile phones,
compared with about
half the European population.
Finland's current 67 percent market
penetration is expected to exceed 70 percent
by the end of the year, a higher rate than in any
other nation. Finland is followed by Hong Kong, Norway,
Sweden, Israel, Japan, Denmark, and Italy in the ranks of top
cellular consumers. Worldwide, mobile phones already surpass
televisions and personal computers combined in terms of unit sales.

(Source: *Los Angeles Times,* Finns out in front in wireless world)

Figure 2.17: Pyramidal Exercise 5 (concluded).

Your training program for improved focused vision can also include exercises where the text is *centered.* In the following exercise, read each line with only one fixation (i.e., the eyes do not move to the right or the left on the line). Your goal is to grasp the essential information in the article. You do not have to understand 100 percent, nor read every word. You are looking for *key* words and *key* concepts. After finishing the article, you need to decide if the contents are of any value to you. If you decide that the information presented is valuable to you, you may want to go through the whole text or part of it again.

Beware of Business Spam

Peek over your cube wall.
That mild-mannered person
sitting next to you might actually be
your e-mail nemesis:
an insidious spammer
who sends out mocking happy faces
in response to office correspondence
and who always selects "reply to all."
That's right, according to
an "occupational spam" study
released Thursday by IT research
company Gartner Group, Inc.,
gratuitous inter-office e-mail
has become a huge problem.
Business e-mailers
intending to send helpful messages
or cover their backs
by copying the entire company
are flooding in-boxes,
straining networks,
wasting heaps of time,
and possibly, mounds of money.
According to Gartner's survey
of 330 business e-mail users,
in primarily U.S. companies
ranging from 20 to 10,000 employees,
42 percent of respondents said
that they are flat-out
getting too much e-mail,
and spend an average of 49 minutes
a day just managing it.
"There's no spam filter in the world
that is going to block this,
which is why it is particularly insidious,"
says Neil MacDonald,
a vice president and
research director with Gartner.

Figure 2.18: Text Centered Exercise 6.

(continued)

McDonald points out
that unlike traditional spam,
which usually comes from strangers
trying to sell you something,
"occupational spam,"
as Gartner researchers call it,
is deceptive because it comes
from people you know and work with.
"This is e-mail
from your friends and colleagues
that is worthless,"
MacDonald says.
To avoid getting bogged down
in mounds of e-mail,
Gartner released
a list of recommendations
that include such helpful tips as
"count to 10 before hitting 'reply all'
then count to 20" and
"assume that agreement is implied...
avoid sending
needless responses of concurrence like
'I'm with you 100 percent.'"
Other more substantial
Gartner advice suggests that
companies invest in intranet tools
for remote team collaboration,
such as chatrooms,
and identify the one person
in the department
who will "own" an e-mail thread
and can communicate
the ideas to co-workers
without copying everyone on e-mail.
By ridding themselves
of occupational spam,
companies can save employees
30 percent of the time
it takes to manage

Figure 2.18: Text Centered Exercise 6 (continued).

their e-mail,
Gartner says.
The research company suggests
that all companies
should have
an e-mail policy in place,
as well as standards
for e-mail etiquette.
But even if companies manage
to shore up the flood
of inter-office e-mail,
another predator still lurks
in the waters:
the constant e-mail checker.
Thirty-four percent of those
surveyed by Gartner reported
that they were checking their e-mail
more than 10 times a day.

(Source: www.ITworld.com)

Figure 2.18: Text Centered Exercise 6 (concluded).

How to Practice on a Computer Screen

It is easy to practice pyramidal methods on a screen. Take a blank piece of 8½" x 11" paper, place it horizontally and draw an even shaped triangle (each side about 8 inches) in the middle. Now cut this triangle out of the paper and attach the paper to your screen with tape. The only text you can now see is through the triangular cut-out. Select a text to practice on your screen (preferably a text in manuscript format without pictures). Slide your guide slowly down the middle of the screen. Expand your vision horizontally by taking in as many words as possible without moving your eyes. Do this exercise at least once a day for 2 to 3 minutes during the first week until you notice that you can take four to six words per fixation.

Start reading the morning paper only one fixation per line. Usually, the columns contain four to eight words, which makes it easy to practice with this technique. You will also notice that less time is spent going through the paper.

Relaxation Exercise B: Palming

You have now trained your peripheral and focused vision. It is time to relax your eyes with "the palming" exercise.

1. Rub your hands together briskly, until the palms are warm.

2. Lean forward on your elbows, cupping your hands over your closed eyes, resting lightly.

3. Concentrate on thinking blackness—something that is black, such as black velvet, a black cat, or a dark night.

4. Rest like this, breath evenly, and count to 60.

5. Open your eyes slowly.

Reading Exercise 3: Take more words at a time. Read the following text or go to the Web page (www.hrdpress.com/effective screenreading/exercises.html). Take advantage of your peripheral and focused vision. Make a conscious effort to take in as many words as you can with each fixation. Your ultimate goal is to read each line with only one fixation. Pull your guide down the middle of the line, concentrate on the text, and keep going forward. Read the text for 1 minute and calculate the number of words based on the 100-word dots in the left margin. Each additional line has six words on average.

Functions such as breathing, thinking, reflexes and memory are all controlled by the central nervous system. It is comprised of highly specialized cells called neurones or nerves. These cells make electrical impulses and transmit them in a similar way to wire carrying electricity. The central nervous system comprises four parts. The brain and spinal cord are the main pathways by which an organism's cells communicate. The receptor cells detect a stimulus, and make up the five senses—sight, smell, touch, taste and hearing. The sensory nerves carry messages from the receptor cells to the

● spine and brain. The motor nerves (/) carry messages to the effectors; these are glands or muscles that respond to a stimulus. A reflex, such as flinching at a pain, is a response to a danger.

Humans have a large brain compared to other mammals. In an adult the brain has about 100 billion neurones. Brain cells cannot be replaced once they are damaged; this is why brain damage is generally permanent. The cerebrum is the movement center of the brain. The area is highly folded, which increases the surface area of its cells and therefore the number of messages that it can process simultaneously. The neurones

● (/) do not touch each other and the gap between them is called the synapse. Impulses cross the gap via neurotransmitters, which are subsequently removed by biological catalysts called enzymes. Some toxins produced by snakes and spiders act by disrupting the enzymes. Over fifty neurotransmitters have been identified. Dopamine is one of them and is responsible for emotional behavior. The brain also produces pain killing neurotransmitters, such as encephalin and endorphins. Heroin and morphine are artificial forms of these neurotransmitters.

- Some drugs act in ways similar to neurotransmitters and are called psychoactive for this reason. Some are legal, such as tobacco, alcohol and prescription drugs. Others, such as heroin and marijuana, are illegal. A person can come to believe that they need a particular drug to function and become psychologically dependent on a drug. The body itself can become physically dependent on a drug. This can occur when the neurotransmitters in the brain become conditioned to the presence of the drug and can't function correctly if the drug is withdrawn. On the other hand, the brain may build up a tolerance to the drug and the user finds that a larger amount of it is required to get the same response.

- Another of the body's message networks is the endocrine network. The endocrine glands include the pituitary glands thyroid gland, pancreas, adrenal glands, and the gonads. These glands produce hormones that lock onto the outside of a target cell and induce a change in that cell. While the pituitary gland produces some hormones, its main role is to direct the other endocrine glands. The thyroid gland produces two hormones involved in the homeostasis of calcium in the blood. Homeostasis is a constant level of a substance in the system; calcitonin removes soluble calcium and stores it in the insoluble form in

- bones, while thyroxin removes it from the bones and returns it to the blood. Pheromones are the chemical messengers used by organisms of the same species to attract a mate. While insects and other mammals are known to use these, no human equivalent has been identified.

The regulation of cellular respiration is controlled by the supply of the simple sugar glucose. After eating, glucose levels in the blood rise. The pancreas excretes insulin to turn the excess glucose into glycogen, which is then stored by the liver. If glucose is consumed during exercise, the pancreas releases glucagons to turn glycogen

- into glucose again. In this way the pancreas maintains homeostasis of glucose levels in the blood.

The regulation of cellular respiration is controlled by the supply of the simple sugar glucose. After eating, glucose levels in the blood rise. The pancreas excretes insulin to turn the excess glucose into glycogen, which is then stored by the liver. If glucose is consumed during exercise, the pancreas releases glucagons to turn glycogen

- into glucose again. In this way the pancreas maintains homeostasis of glucose levels in the blood.

In general, diabetes is caused by the destruction of the cells in the pancreas that produce insulin. Insulin-dependent diabetics must inject themselves daily with the hormone and follow a strict diet and exercise plan. This helps them avoid hypoglycemia, where the blood sugar level drops dramatically. The treatment used to avoid confusion, shaking or coma is to give the sufferer some sugar. Prior to 1980, the insulin used to treat diabetics was extracted from the pancreases of cows and pigs.

- Today, the insulin is produced in bulk from genetically engineered bacteria. Other treatments include the implantation of donor pancreases, or the pancreas of a genetically altered pig. The other option is to inject the cells responsible for insulin production. If another type of cell can be induced to produce insulin, they can be introduced then into the pancreas to replace the destroyed cells.

The kidneys are responsible for removing most of the waste produced by the body. Urea is the broken down amino acids produced by the liver. The kidney treats this to conserve water, salts, glucose, and complete amino
- acids, while removing toxic waste. Kidneys are involved in maintaining the homeostasis of water and salts in the body and can produce more concentrate or dilute urine to do so. Illness, injury, or overuse of some drugs can cause kidney failure. While a human can survive with the use of one fully functioning kidney, anything less would require the person to undergo dialysis

two to four times a week. Dialysis is when a machine is used to perform the same function as the kidneys. It takes approximately four hours, and most people on dialysis live in hope of a kidney transplant.

- Reptiles and insects are ectodermic—the external environment regulates their body temperature. Mammals, birds and fish are endotherms, maintaining a stable body temperature through internal metabolism. The human body needs to stay around 37°C, and hypothermia will result if the temperature drops dramatically. On the other hand, an elevated body temperature causes hyperthermia. The body cools itself by sweating, or through vasodilatation. The blood vessels close to the skin expand to increase the volume of blood flowing through and so heat is lost to the environment. Heat is generated through shivering, vasorestriction or through goose bumps. Goose bumps raise the
- hair on the skin, trapping warm air between fur and skin. On relatively hairless humans, this contributes little to heat generation.

Plants also respond to stimuli, but in a simpler fashion. These responses are called tropisms. Phototropism is the response to light—this helps the plant to measure the length of the day, and hence flower or die at the correct time of year. Gravitropism is the response to gravity—when a seed germinates it needs to point its roots down and its shoots up. The hormone responsible

- for this is called auxin. For example, it causes cells on the dark side of the plant to elongate, so bending the plant to the light source. A plant will remove all food from a leaf, and transfer waste there before releasing a growth-inhibiting hormone to cause the leaf to drop off. The gas ethylene is involved in the ripening of fruit, so fruit can be picked before it ripens and is caused to do so at a more desirable time. (©bbc.co.uk)

Total number of words in 1 minute: _____

Please enter your result in the reading progression chart in Figure 2.23 at the end of Chapter 2 and subjectively estimate your understanding (Very well, Well, Sufficiently, or Little).

Right Brain Technique:
Use Maximum Brain Capacity

The business world is constantly changing. Companies come and go, small companies merge into bigger organizations, and big companies downsize into smaller, independent entities. Totally new branches of businesses emerge, especially in the field of information technology where virtual companies, with the help of the Internet, can market their products globally from headquarters located anywhere in the world. Technologies develop rapidly while life spans of new products become shorter and shorter.

For the human being, it is difficult to adapt to these changes as fast as is required in this hectic environment; certainly the human anatomy or physical shape cannot be changed. It has taken a few million years for the human being to develop into its present state, while the modern human brain has taken around 50,000 years to evolve to its current level. Therefore, a time span of only 10 to 20 years is simply not recognized in evolutionary terms. However, in the information industry, even five years seems to be forever.

Consequently, it is reasonable to assume that no major evolutionary changes will affect the human eyes and brain in the foreseeable future. So we will all have to get on with what we have, how it works, and how it is constructed. However, by knowing how the brain works, you can adjust your habits and skills to support its natural way of functioning. This will lead to a higher efficiency in everything you become involved in. When managing the huge flow of electronic information, this efficiency results in improved reading speed and comprehension.

The Theory of the Left-Right Hemispheres of the Brain

According to the theory and research by Professor Roger Sperry of California, the two sides, or hemispheres, of the brain tend to divide the major intellectual tasks between them. This research work by Sperry was so highly admired in the world of science that he was awarded the Nobel Prize in 1981.

Figure 2.19 demonstrates a transaxial image of the human brain, mainly the upper part that is called the *cortex* (cerebral cortex). It is only 3 to 5 mm thick and contains most of the brain cells. The cortex of the brain is an area where most of the intellectual thinking, planning, problem solving, and decision making take place. It is possible to distinguish two separate sides or hemispheres—the left and the right. These are connected with intricate bundles of fibers called *corpus callosum*. Each side has separate, but not unique capabilities. According to Sperry, the left side, i.e., the "analytical" part of the brain, can process letters, words, numbers, order, logic, and linearity. The right side, i.e., the "artistic" part of the brain, deals with such intellectual areas as rhythm, overview, imagination, space, colors, daydreaming, etc. Most of the time during reading, people use only the skills located in the left side. This is partly the reason why their speed will only vary around 200 words per minute.

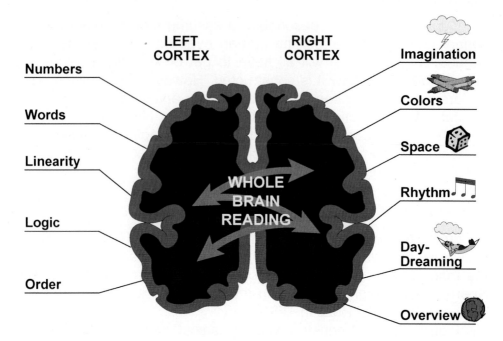

By utilizing both sides of the brain, reading speeds of 400 to 4,000 words per minute are possible.

Figure 2.19: Whole brain reading.

However, by utilizing both the left and the right sides of the brain together, you do not just double your reading ability and skills. Rather, with this combined power, the synergy between the two hemispheres makes its sum higher than the individual parts alone, and your ability makes a quantum leap.

Combine the correct use of the eyes, both sides of the brain, and "the tool kit" (that is, the concrete techniques), and your ability to manage e-mails and Web pages will reach levels that you could not have imagined before.

The most recent scientific investigation has shown that as the left part of the brain operates on β-frequencies (i.e., the electric frequency at which the brain normally operates when we are awake), the right side of the brain can stay at α-frequencies (relaxed state of mind). In this capacity, the right hemisphere acts more in the nature of assisting and monitoring the left side.

One should be aware that the actual visual perception from the environment does not always exactly match with the information that is conveyed to the brain from the eyes. Even though some objects in certain lighting conditions emit light back to our eyes differently, we will still recognize them and their original colors. The brain does not accept the information from the eyes as such, but tends to treat this data further and change the actual visual perception according to some pre-assumptions. Therefore the visual capability cannot only be accredited to the excellent optics of the eyes, but it involves a great deal of information processing and continuous analysis carried out by the brain.

Where is the connection between the visual capability, the theory of the two brain hemispheres, and the increased efficiency in front of a computer terminal? Could we in some way benefit from current brain research? The following paragraphs and exercises will reveal the answers.

When reading from a computer screen, it is obvious that many of the skills located in the left hemisphere are used. These are the skills that you have been taught to use traditionally with any written material and that you naturally use every day in front of computer terminals.

How could you start using and benefit from the skills in the right hemisphere?

The skills or activities located in the right side of the brain are often referred to as "artistic" or "creative." Therefore many people consider them to be difficult to practice and utilize with computers. However, these skills can assist in your reading in a very positive way. We will show how to use two of them: rhythm and imagination (mind setting).

Rhythm

Children are normally taught to read at a certain "comfortable" speed at school. If later they try to increase this speed, they often feel that the comprehension will drop and the reading activity as such will become strenuous. Especially long, difficult, boring, or overly interesting texts can result in a gradual slowing down of the speed over time.

However, the use of a *metronome* will add an extra skill to your reading armory. You can benefit from a metronome in two ways: increasing your speed gradually or reading super fast. Each beat may indicate a single stroke along the line of the text. Every stroke signifies the speed.

An example will illustrate this.

If your normal speed is 180 wpm, you may set the metronome to pulse 30 bpm (beats per minute), which keeps the beat to read 180 wpm (6 words per line on an average). Practice reading with your normal speed for 5 minutes and then add an extra two or three beats more. Your speed will then be around 200 wpm. Read again for 5 minutes with this new speed and then add some beats. It is important that your increments are modest in order to achieve your objectives.

In this way, an improved, steady, smooth reading rhythm will be achieved, and back-skipping as well as deceleration will be avoided. You can also increase the speed by varying it, first to super fast and then "slow" down again. A couple of weeks will be enough to notice an improvement, not only in your speed, but also in comprehension.

There is a correlation between fitness, heart beat, and reading speed. Generally speaking, the rhythm used with reading should support the natural rhythm of your body, i.e., your body's natural pulsation (heartbeats per minute). When at rest, the heart pulsates at 60 to 70 beats per minute (bpm), with some less physically fit people up to 70 to 90 bpm, and more athletic people between 40 to 60 bpm. If you read one line per second, and each line contains on an average 10 words, your speed is 600 wpm, i.e., 60 lines per minute. If the text has 6 words per line, you should set the metronome at 100, which means roughly two lines per second. By maintaining this speed, your reading will become more disciplinary and the right side of your brain will be involved.

Compare reading with athletics. When jogging or swimming, if you maintain a constant, steady speed, you will not get nearly as tired as you would if you varied the speed all the time. Search for a speed that is in line with your body's natural functioning. For many of us, this is around 600 to 800 wpm.

A good example of a famous speed reader was John F. Kennedy, who was able to read double the heart beat, i.e., around 1,200 wpm. This equates to 120 lines per minute with each line containing on average 10 words. His comprehension was so high that he was able to make instant summaries to his staff about virtually everything he had read.

The second major application of the metronome training method is based on the "relativistic" nature of the brain. This means that when performing the same task over and over again, the brain will get used to doing this operation in a certain way. As people are used to reading at a certain speed, it would be interesting to see if this level could be raised one step higher and kept there.

The following exercise illustrates how to benefit from a metronome.

Set the metronome at a super high speed (for example 100 bpm) and practice reading at that speed for about 5 minutes. Just look at the words and let them pour into your head. "Forget" understanding!

To practice, read the previous text (Reading Exercise 3) again from the start to the finish (from the book or from our Web pages) by setting your metronome to 100 bpm. Use a CS guide to assist your eyes. Force your eye/brain system to become accustomed to this new, super speed in order to establish a new, very high norm.

After the 5-minute time period, you can return back to your normal "safe" speed. If you now measure your reading speed, you will find that your "normal" reading speed is actually faster than before. The brain "got used to" the high speed and actually has difficulties slowing down. This is a good example of how to take advantage of the relativistic nature of the human brain.

Imagination and Mind Setting

When you start reading something long and time consuming, for example, a multi-page operating manual, it is very important to think about the topic beforehand and imagine the subject matter in the form of a picture. This technique is called *applied imagination* or *mind setting*. Concentrating your thoughts on the subject, before studying or reading about it, will accelerate the actual learning process and make it more enjoyable. You will also go through the material faster. Using your imagination—creating a picture in your mind—will make it easier to attach new, detailed information to the existing database already in your mind. This technique will also significantly improve your memory. Starting from the overall picture and proceeding then to details will enhance adult learning in most cases. The opposite is true, however, for children—they normally start from the details and try to form the complete view from small pieces of information.

Follow these steps when using applied imagination (have a pen and a piece of white paper available).

1. Before you start to read, pause and close your eyes.

2. In a few seconds, try to create an image about the topic of the book, report, project, etc., in your mind. What type of form, dimension, and colors would you give it?

3. Make a quick drawing of this image in the middle of the paper.

4. Draw 10 lines to this central image and write or draw on top of each line what first comes into your mind about the topic—what image.

If more things come to your mind, continue adding lines or sub-lines to the first 10 lines you already drew. Write or draw the things popping in to your mind on these lines.

You have now created a picture in your mind about the subject. The old saying that "a picture is worth a thousand words" is quite true here. You have opened the door for the new information to become more easily connected to this mental picture. Applied imagination will create the fundamental basis for learning and remembering, where the key is the readiness and smooth flow of new things to become attached to the existing database that you already know.

Applied imagination will help focus your mind on the topic. People often think that they don't know anything or only very little about a new subject to be studied. After using mind setting, they are quite amazed about the amount of information already stored in their minds. By focusing your thoughts, you can devote less time to those parts of the text that you previously know and concentrate on more valuable topics. New information is easy to attach to the old one when a clear, overall picture of the subject exists beforehand. This will also enhance future recall.

Relaxation Exercise C: The Melting Snowman

It is time again to relax your mind. The following exercise will lower the frequency of the brain waves close to the alpha range. It combines both hemispheres at the same time for deep relaxation and can be done in front of your computer screen.

1. With your eyes closed, imagine a snowman standing in spring sunshine.

2. Keep this picture as clear and vivid as possible in your mind and start counting backward from 60 to 0.

3. With each count, see your snowman slowly melting.

4. By the time you reach 0, your snowman has totally melted away and is merely a puddle of water on the ground.

Before reading the text of the next reading exercise, use the technique of applied imagination and think about what you already know about the topic *cholesterol* (see Figure 2.20).

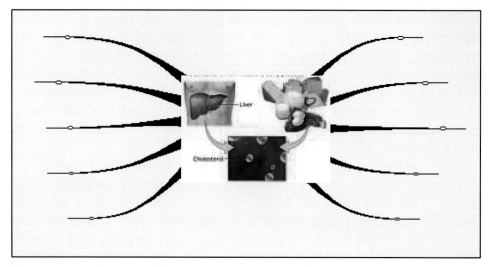

(Source: www.bio.owu.edu)

Figure 2.20: How to use applied imagination and mind setting: Cholesterol.

Reading Exercise 4: Use rhythm and applied imagination. Read the following text or go to the Web page (www.hrdpress.com/effectivescreenreading/exercises.html). Try to read to a fast, steady beat. Take a look at the heading. Imagine a picture in your mind about the topic. Use your visual capability and take large chunks of words per each fixation. Use your guide, keep your concentration 100 percent on the text, and *move forward only*. Read that text for 1 minute and calculate the number of words based on the 100-word dots in the left margin.

People who significantly cut their cholesterol levels with statins may raise the risk of cancer, a study says. The study of 40,000 people found those with little of the "bad" cholesterol LDL saw one more cancer case per 1,000 than those with higher levels. The Boston-based researchers could not say if this was a side-effect of the statin or due to the low cholesterol. They also write in the Journal of the American College of Cardiology that the benefits of statins outweigh the risks.

- "The analysis doesn't implicate the statin in creasing the risk of cancer," says lead author Richard Karas of Tufts University School of Medicine in Boston. "The demonstrated benefits of statins in lowering the risk of heart disease remain clear. However certain aspects of lowering LDL with statins remain controlversial and merit further research." Researchers looked at the summary data from 13 trials of people taking statins—a total of 41,173 patients. These findings do not change the message that the benefits of taking statins greatly outweigh any potential risks. British Heart Foundation examined the relationship between low, medium and high doses of statins and
- rates of newly diagnosed cancer. Higher rates of the disease—which were not of any type or location—were observed in the group with the lower levels. The authors noted their findings

were particularly important at a time when more and more trials show significant reductions in LDL levels can greatly benefit cardiovascular health.

Cancer information officer Dr. Alison Ross said: "The findings of this study should be treated with caution—it is based on summary data from previous trials and, as the authors point out themselves, it does not prove that low LDL cholesterol levels can increase cancer risk. Much more research is needed before any firm conclusions can be made." The British Heart Foundation said they had long known of a relationship between low cholesterol and cancer. "While this highlights an association between low levels of LDL and cancer, this is not the same as saying that low LDL or statin use increases the risk of cancer," said June Davison, cardiac nurse. "There is overwhelming evidence that lowering LDL cholesterol through statins saves lives by preventing heart attacks and strokes. These findings do not change the message that the benefits of taking statins greatly outweigh any potential risks."

- A major international trial has been set up to see whether a treatment to increase so-called "good" cholesterol can prevent heart attacks and strokes. "Good" cholesterol—high density lipoproteins (HDL)—cuts heart disease risk by removing fat from the circulation. The treatment, designed to increase levels of HDL, will be given alongside drugs to reduce "bad" cholesterol,

alongside drugs to reduce "bad" cholesterol, which can raise the risk of disease. A team at Oxford University is leading the trial involving 20,000 volunteers. To be eligible for the trial, patients must be aged between 50 and 80 with a history of heart attack, stroke or peripheral artery disease. Around

- 7,500 men and women will be recruited from the UK with people from China and Scandinavia making up the rest of the participants. The main ingredient in the trial drug is niacin, which has been found to increase levels of HDL by between a fifth and a quarter as well as decreasing dangerous fatty substances called triglycerides. "The trial will be in people at risk of future heart problems despite the fact that their LDL cholesterol has been lowered," said Dr. Jane Armitage, trial leader.

- But patients have found it difficult to take niacin long-term because it produces an uncomfortable side-effect of flushing. To combat this effect, niacin has been combined with another drug, which blocks the release of prostaglandin D2—the substance which produces the flushing effect. The team at the Clinical Trials Unit at Oxford previously carried out the landmark Heart Protection Study which showed a third of all heart attacks and strokes could be avoided in people at risk of vascular disease by using statins to lower "bad" cholesterol or low density lipoproteins (LDL). Large-scale trials have shown that lowering LDL for four to five years cuts the risk of heart attacks and stroke

- by a quarter. But the risk among

patients who already have vascular disease remains high even with the use of statins and there is limited scope for reducing LDL much more, so researchers are starting to look at ways of also increasing HDL.

Dr. Jane Armitage who is leading the trial said: "The difficulty has been that there haven't been good quality drugs that raise HDL very much. The trial will be in people at risk of future heart problems despite the fact that their LDL cholesterol has been lowered. If it's

• shown to work, the epidemiology suggests it will be possible for people at lower risk of heart problems to benefit."

Professor Gilbert Thompson, a lipidology expert at Imperial College said treatments which raise HDL were the "next step" in cholesterol research. "It seems a perfectly reasonable approach but it won't necessarily give you a straight answer about HDL because niacin also lowers triglyceride. But it will be a good trial. Dr. Anthony Wierzbicki, Chair of Heart UK Scientific Medical and Research Committee, said looking for ways of raising HDL in addition to lowering LDL was the next logical step.

• "There are a number of trials looking at this that are either under way or starting soon, all following the protocol of adding HDL-raising agents to baseline statin therapy in a variety of patient populations." A group of drugs called CETP inhibitors have also been shown to increase levels of "good" cholesterol and are currently in clinical trials.

Effective Screen Reading

Total number of words in 1 minute: _____

Please enter the result in the reading progression chart in Figure 2.24 at the end of Chapter 2 and subjectively estimate your understanding (Very well, Well, Sufficiently, and Little).

PDS Technique: Set Yourself Correctly

Take into consideration the next three areas, and your capacity to read efficiently will be greatly improved:

1. Position and posture in front of the computer
2. Distance to the screen
3. Mental ability to feel strong during the reading process

Thus, the acronym PDS comes from position, distance, and strength.

Position

Make your position in front of the computer as comfortable as possible. Release any tight garments and shoes. If possible, lean back a little bit but hold your posture and back straight. Loosen up any stiffness you might have in your neck and shoulder muscles to achieve a relaxed feeling.

There are three easy-to-remember rules of thumb to become relaxed. These are the same basic principles, as applied in aikido, one of the oldest Japanese martial arts.

1. **Do one thing at a time.** You should pay attention only to your reading task. If you have to do other things simultaneously, like answering the phone or signing letters, you will not only drastically slow down your reading speed but also increase the tension in the muscles. Eliminate distractions and remember to take breaks. Keeping your mind concentrated on the task will greatly enhance your efficiency.

2. **Drop down your internal center of gravity.** People normally maintain their internal balance—internal center of gravity—in the upper part of the body—in the upper back, shoulder, or neck area. This is the area where most tension is accumulated. However, just by looking at the body, you

can notice that the center point is located somewhere around the waist area. Consequently, keep reminding yourself to lower the balance by consciously dropping any tension you may have in the shoulder area as low as possible.

3. **Become relaxed.** When you succeed in the above two principles, you will automatically notice that the body becomes more relaxed. As the internal balance drops down, the tension from the shoulder and neck area will gradually disappear.

Distance

The capacity of your peripheral vision is not only sufficient to take in the entire screen but also the surrounding environment both at the same time. The eyes do not capture the page starting from the upper left hand corner like they would do when reading a book. On the contrary, the image of the page is transferred to the brain with one global shot in a fraction of a second. Therefore, when you go through Web pages, you are actually *re*reading things already seen.

The optimal reading distance to the computer screen depends on multiple variables. Besides peripheral vision, other factors need to be considered in order to achieve the most efficient reading conditions for highest comprehension. These include the following:

- reader's vision ability—good "screen vision"
- the size, type, and layout of the text
- the lighting and contrast
- the quality of the equipment

In this chapter, we will deal with the first topic, the visual capability. The three others are explained in detail in Chapter 3.

The ability to see clearly is without doubt the major factor in determining the distance between the reader and the screen. By good "screen vision," we mean the following:

- the capability to focus the eyes sharply on the text and to see the pictures clearly

- a sufficient field of vision to perceive the whole screen with one glance and to make detailed observations even from the margins of a larger monitor

- vision for contrasts and darkness—ability to perceive shades of gray

- tolerance for glare—ability to compensate flickering of the screen or sudden reflections of light coming from the monitor

- dynamic depth vision to compensate the changing of reading distance during the working day

If you sit too close, you will loose the advantages of peripheral vision, and the text itself may become blurred. On the other hand, if the screen is too far away, you may encounter difficulties seeing the words clearly, or you may not be able to use your CS guide.

Using eyeglasses may sometimes create confusion. For near-sighted people, using eyeglasses for reading a book is in most cases not necessary. However, for these people, if eyeglasses are not used and the screen is positioned farther than 16 to 20 inches away from them, the text on the screen might become blurred. For those who are far-sighted and use eyeglasses only when reading books, the text on the screen is often seen clearly without glasses. Significant differences exist from individual to individual, and the optimum solution can only be found by trial and error.

If you strain your eyes when working at your computer terminal, the recommendation is to use eyeglasses all the time. The lack of or wrong type of eyeglasses may cause headaches and eye fatigue, especially when sitting at a computer for a prolonged period of time. Remember to clean your eyeglasses before starting a reading task.

When reading a book, it is recommended to have it at arm's length. This will allow the full benefit of the peripheral vision. However, the screen should be positioned farther away because the screen text size is bigger than that used in books. Fonts normally used are 10 or 12 points, although these will be most often enlarged by the selected display resolution. The screen should be at least *twice* as far away from your eyes as you would normally hold a book. If you hold a book at a distance of 14 inches, your screen should be positioned at least 28 inches away.

Resolution of the display. The desktop display may have an immediate impact on your visual capability. The resolution of the screen is indicated as the total number of pixels on the display or as the number of pixels per square inch. A *pixel* is an individual picture unit, which comprises three main colors: red, blue, and green. The resolution of a 15-inch monitor typically is 1,024 x 768—it has 1,024 pixels horizontally and 768 pixels vertically. This results in just under 100 pixels per square inch. To change the resolution, click *Control Panel, Display, Settings,* or right click the mouse over desktop and select *Properties, Settings.*

Depending on the monitor, the alternatives normally available are listed below:

- 800 x 600
- 1,024 x 768
- 1,280 x 1,024
- 1,400 x 1,050

Pixel ratio of 1,600 x 1,200 can also be found, but it is rarely used. It is worthwhile to test different configurations, because a higher pixel ratio means sharper—more readable—text. However, a high resolution does not automatically guarantee the best end result, because the text becomes smaller and more difficult to read. Your eyes will get tired if you have to constantly stare at text that is too small. Here a larger type font may offer some help.

Grouping of words. Trained eyes can focus on 4 to 10 words at the same time. This capability of grouping words is fundamental in digital reading and the selected distance to the screen should always support this. Both Web pages and e-mails contain lines, the lengths of which are normally only 5 to 10 words. Therefore only two, maximum three, stops are required on each line; with training, one stop is enough.

Mental Strength

Never underestimate the power of your mind. The human brain has a strong attraction to those things it can anticipate. The brain strives to make them become reality. Therefore when you confront a reading task, your ability to feel mentally strong can make a positive difference not only to the total reading time, but to your comprehension as well.

If you think in advance that reading the text will take a long time, be of no use to you, be a boring task, result in quickly forgetting everything, or make you feel sleepy, then this will undoubtedly happen!

However, if you think in advance that reading the material will benefit you greatly, be a pleasurable experience, will—with repetition—stay in your memory for a long time, and keep you alert and interested, then these things will happen!

E-triangle for the Screen Reader

Three areas are interconnected, as shown in Figure 2.21, when managing information on the computer screen:

1. Encephalon
2. Emotions
3. Equipment

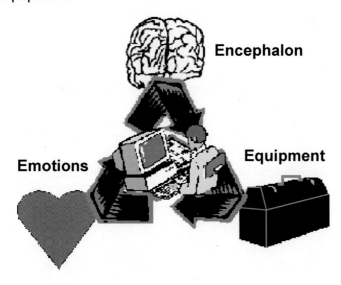

Figure 2.21: E-triangle for the screen reader.

Techniques for Effective Screen Reading

Encephalon (the brain). This is the medical term for the whole brain. According to Paul McLean, an American scientist and the developer of the triune brain theory, the encephalon can be divided into three parts: neocortex, limbic system, and brain stem.

The cortex of the brain is divided into left and right hemispheres. Earlier we explained that the operating frequency in the right side of the brain is more tuned to the α-activity, while the left side has more β-activity. Combine the traditional, academic skills in the left hemisphere with the artistic abilities in the right side and you will be effectively using whole brain reading technique. You will process e-mails, Web pages, and any other electronic text by utilizing all the skills and both frequencies (α- and β-frequencies) available in the brain. This constitutes the essential foundation for a true digital reader.

To maximize the use of your brain:

1. Have a clear vision both in your personal and professional lives. Define your problems and goals clearly—preferably in writing.

2. Have a notepad (or an electronic notebook) always available. Write down ideas when they come to you immediately to avoid clogging the memory.

3. Exercise your brain with daydreaming and fantasy.

4. Set aside time for daily relaxation and meditation.

5. Create variety in your life—become interested in various topics.

6. Always get an overview on new matters first and then build structure.

Emotions

Have your emotions involved, as this will greatly enhance the capability to remember any topic in question. Emotions reside in the limbic (central) part of the brain. They carry strong associations and experiences, which in turn help the memory recall items even though a very long time period has elapsed. Emotions include appreciation, feedback, listening, and taking into consideration others, self-esteem, love, passion, as well as empathy (sincerity and genuineness).

Equipment (Tool Kit)

Your personal equipment—your tool kit—contains all those digital reading techniques that you have learned and that should be used when confronting a reading task. These are your tools. Use them actively!

Firmly believe in your capability and say to yourself before starting any reading assignment: "I am strong and I can easily manage this text with good comprehension in no time at all."

Relaxation Exercise D: Drop Your Internal Gravity

It is time for a relaxation exercise.

1. Concentrate on doing the following reading exercise. Exclude other thoughts.

2. In your mind, drop your internal gravity point below your waistline.

3. Let yourself become relaxed.

Reading Exercise 5: Sit comfortably, feel strong, and adjust your distance. Read the following text or go to the Web page (www.hrdpress.com/effectivescreenreading/exercises.html). Find yourself a truly comfortable position, take off your shoes, optimize your distance from the computer—not too close, not too far—and imagine that you are the "strongest" reader in the world.

Remember to do the following:

- Keep a fast, steady beat.
- Make a picture about the topic—*computer applications*—in your mind.
- Take large chunks of words, preferably one line at a time.
- Use your guide.
- Move forward only.

Read the text for 1 minute and calculate the number of words based on the 100-word dots in the left margin.

Reading Exercise 5: Computer Applications and Innovations

Computer systems are being used in every area of modern society. Computers are everywhere—they tell us how much money we have in our bank account and let us pay for our groceries using a bank card that has a magnetic strip. We can also send our friends messages through the computer electronic mailing system (e-mail). Think about when you borrow from the library. Don't you use the computerized catalogues to find the right book? Anywhere you look, you will see the influence and work of a computer—in art, business, school or entertainment. Computers allow us to go about many daily tasks in a speedy and efficient manner. This is very useful in a fast paced society as ours.

Credit cards have changed the way in which we handle our money. Today, your cash savings can be simply a series of numbers stored in the bank's computer. In the United States, over thirty billion checks are used each year to transfer approximately eight trillion dollars from one group or individual to another. The cost of processing these checks is more than five billion dollars a year for the bank fees alone.

Because of this, a new system has been developed using a computer network to replace much of the check and cash handling. This network allows funds to be transferred directly from one bank account to another via the electronic funds transfer system (EFTS). Some people call this development the "cashless society." It simply means that it will be a society with fewer checks and less cash being used to buy things. Checks take about two to five days to process. The EFTS system allows funds to process within seconds using computers. The system also allows quick reporting on consumer spending habits for Governments

• making connected policies. It is also much easier and safer for the individual to carry a card around instead of large amounts of cash. The EFTS purchase is easy. Imagine that you are going shopping at the mall and need to buy groceries from the supermarket and clothes from a clothing boutique. You go into the supermarket, select your items and take them to the checkout person who would scan the goods through with an electric scanner. Each item is automatically identified by the barcode and the cost will come up on the register. You decide to pay by EFTS and give the shop assistant your

• bank card, who then swipes it through a terminal. You enter the account you are transferring the funds from (savings, check or credit), and enter your personal identification number (PIN) into the EFTS terminal. The bank code on the card dials your account number, checks you have enough money and then transfers those funds into the supermarket's account. The shop you are buying your clothes from doesn't have EFTS terminals, so you decide to take an extra one hundred dollars cash

• out of your account, using the same system. There are many advantages of EFTS. It reduces the amount of cash people must carry—possibly avoiding robbery and loss. It also reduces the amount of cash that shops must keep in their registers. All this would not be possible without computers.

• Computer networks can also be used to enable people to communicate in new ways that combine the advantages of mail and the telephone. Consider mail as a form of communication. It can be carefully written before it is sent to make sure that it says clearly what you want it to say. It can be written when-ever you wish. You can read your e-mail when you have the time available. Both the sender and receiver can have copies of the mail for future reference. However, a letter could take days to deliver, could get lost, or could be delivered to the wrong address. The telephone is a faster form of communi-cation as each person can respond to questions directly expressed by the other person. However, it is often diffi-cult to call at a convenient time. The caller may be interrupting important work or relaxation time of the person being called. That is why e-mail is an exciting invention that overcomes the problems of the other forms of commu-nication.

• E-mail is short for "electronic mail." If both people are connected to a com-puter network, they can communicate in a way that has the advantages of both mail and telephone. People belonging to this system have a reserved area of memory (called a mailbox) within the network. Each person has a different mailbox address. To send a message, you only have to sit down at the computer terminal, type out the address of the receiver, followed by your message. The computer then transfers the message to the receiver's mailbox. If your name is "John Smith," your mailbox might be called something like "jsmith@pobox.com." This is called your e-mail address.

Imagine that you needed to get an important message to your school teacher, but they weren't answering their phone. If you knew their e-mail address, you could leave a message and they could get back to you at anytime. Very convenient, don't you think? The good thing about electronic mail is that the receiver can read it at his/her own leisure. E-mail is much faster than normal mail. Messages arrive in a few seconds after they are sent, instead of days later. Even if you have a friend who lives in another country. You can send him/her an e-mail and it might take only a few minutes to send! You can either store your mail or erase it after reading it. Computers and the Internet have made this type of communication a reality.

There are computer techniques that allow us to store and find information quickly. Database software allows large amounts of information to be stored and retrieved in many different ways. This is of great use to students, scientists, and companies who need to find information. These type of techniques are already being used in public, state

● and school libraries, making it easier to obtain access to information hidden somewhere on the library shelves. Obviously, librarians would have been concerned with how to arrange information in a way that will be easier to find when needed. Books are usually catalogued according to their general subject area, as well as by title and author. Each book is given a catalogue number that specifies where the book can be found within the library. So, if you know the book's title or author you can look it up in the catalogue to see where it's stored. But if you are inter-

● ested in finding a book in a general subject area like on environmental problems, it will give you a large list of the books to be found within that area.

The computer makes this system easier by getting rid of the card catalogues and replacing them with a magnetic disk which holds the same information. So, you could then sit at a computer terminal and type in the title, author or general area. The computer will then flash all the information on the screen, until you direct it to give you more specific details on one book. You then write

● down the catalogue number and go find the book.

However, think about the times you might have used this system—did the computer list about 100 different titles on environmental pollution (for example), yet it could not tell you which

books dealt with water pollution and chemicals? More sophisticated systems have many keywords describing the subject matter of a book. Then the computer can find a short list on the specific topics typed in by the user. For example, you could type in "water pollution," "poisons," and "published after 1985," and the computer would list the few books that meet those conditions. This would save you the time and effort of reading through the titles of many books on a general topic. It also saves you from rushing to the shelves to get a book whose title is misleading and contains nothing that you need. So we see that computers, with clever database software, can allow people to obtain easier and quicker access to a wide range of materials that they need. Research for school assignments or other book-requiring activities, will become a task that should take less time and effort.

Another useful link between computers and learning is that of computer-assisted instruction which can help students master mathematics, vocabulary and language skills. For example, for mathematics, a computer can present problems and wait until the student types in the answer. If the answer is correct the computer will give another problem. If it is wrong the computer will get the student to work through the problem again. You could do the same thing for grammar, typing and other subjects. The introduction of home correspondence courses and self-study courses will be possible through this computer technology. (©bbc.co.uk)

Total number of words in 1 minute: _____

Please enter your result in the reading progression chart in Figure 2.24 at the end of Chapter 2 and subjectively estimate your understanding (Very well, Well, Sufficiently, or Little).

Turbo Technique

Changing Habits

When employees meet informally with each other and exchange opinions in organizations, new intangible information is created. This "silent" information is normally not registered anywhere else than in the minds of those involved and is therefore called *tacit knowledge*. It includes the skills, beliefs, values, and habits hidden in their minds. How to profit from tacit knowledge is one of the major questions for company management.

The experience of employees has a great impact on generating tacit knowledge that in the course of time will turn into a collective "organizational memory." This type of memory is the result of intuition or feelings. A statement such as "It seems to me as if..." is part of it. Speechless knowledge is most often connected to certain situations and habits, and people then act accordingly.

In the beginning of Chapter 2, we presented statements on how reading should and should not be done. Many of these ideas reflect the habits formed during formal education, which are then transferred to professional lives.

Changing habits is difficult. You are accustomed to doing things in a certain way and to learn a new way may seem impossible. You might have tried to make a change, failed, and decided, Why bother? A short story on prejudices is worth telling.

Be Aware of Prejudices

An owner of a fish-hatching center had in one of his water tanks a huge shark—a devil of a shark. In the same tank, he also had some smaller fish swimming around. Whenever the devil shark became hungry, it caught a defenseless fish and ate it. The owner thought that the shark was having life too easy, and one night he placed a transparent divider in the tank separating the shark from the smaller fish. The next morning when the shark woke up feeling hungry, it immediately tried to catch a small fish. However, it collided against the separator, hitting its head. The shark tried again with the same result. Having hit itself some 10 times, it swam into the corner of the tank and started to mope.

During the next three days, the physical condition of the devil shark deteriorated due to lack of nutrition. The owner started to feel pity for his shark and removed the separator. However, the devil shark continued moping and did not move from the corner. What do you think happened to the shark after 10 days of moping in the corner? Of course, it died! What was the reason for its death? Hunger and lack of food maybe... Wrong! The shark died of prejudices. "I have tried to catch those fish before without success. No reason to try again."

Sometimes employees feel the same way as the shark when they are trying to manage the excessive information flow. However, if you use effective reading tools, you don't have to remain in the corner like the shark, when facing this mass of information. Make a conscious change that is based on scientific research and unconditionally accept that the new digital reading tools will benefit you in your life. When you become convinced that it is possible to read any electronic text faster and understand it better, it is time to start practicing the available techniques systematically. This new behavior will support the belief itself that in turn will help the behavior. Inevitably, a positive "snowball effect" is created. Figuratively speaking, swim out from the corner and start catching the small fish again!

New techniques may initially slow you down, as it naturally will take some time to learn them. You might feel tempted to go back to your old style, which is familiar, safe, effortless, and easy to remember, and presents no risks. Your new (digital reading) techniques are easy to forget, are sometimes hard to practice, require extra effort, and might even present risks. New memory patterns formed in the brain are also very weak and fragile, because they are not yet well connected and associated. They need repetition and elaboration to develop the associations that make them strong.

The past (or old habits), the present, and the future (or new habits) are interconnected. Old habits are derived from the past and stored in the cortex of the brain. It is now (today) that you make the decisions affecting your future. New habits are like "memories of the future." You must make the decision to abandon some old habits and start using new ones. Your decision today affects your performance and behavior in the future. The future includes action programs, short- and long-term planning, goal setting, formulating visions, and setting expectations.

Once you have made the decision to adopt new habits in your everyday reading, you should immediately start practicing these tried and tested techniques. From now on, you should remind yourself to use them actively on whatever you read and at all times. "Move forward only. Use the guide. Keep on the page...." should be subconsciously repeated in order to establish the new habit more permanently in your memory. The repetition will make it a routine, thus increasing its stability. Anything extra that will connect the new habit more and more firmly to your everyday reading assignments is encouraged. Should you find yourself in the middle of some reading task and not using these new techniques, do not get totally upset. With positive thinking and conscious self-discipline, refocus your efforts and get back to the already established new habit, because it needs to be built up to become stronger.

Three aspects top the list, when establishing new habits. These are belief, practice and motivation.

1. **Belief.** You should believe that speeds between 600 to 1,000 words per minute are both possible and achievable. You just need the brain to work with the eyes and use this magnificent equipment properly. You will easily override

any old myths and misconceptions that normally limit and slow down the reading speed. "I can!" will be your motto. However, belief alone is not enough. You also need to practice and be motivated to make the change.

2. **Practice.** New skills should be honed and perfected on a daily basis. Just knowing about them is not enough. Compared to learning other useful skills (playing an instrument, learning how to draw, etc.), the best part in your new digital reading skills is that to practice them you do not have to set aside any extra time (except in the very beginning). You can use them with your daily reading routines (reports, memorandums, magazines, etc.). This continuous training will strengthen your new memory traces and desired new habits.

3. **Motivation.** You must have a genuine desire to make a conscious change. You have to be motivated, because this will stimulate the brain activity for improved awareness. Motivation helps you sit straighter, breath more freely and deeper, organize and prepare yourself better for work, etc. All these will enhance your ability to adopt the new habit faster.

Any one of these three areas *alone* is not enough. Bear in mind that changing old habits often encounters a strong, internal resistance. However, as your knowledge about the functioning of the eye-brain combination has increased, you can make a *conscious decision* to change from a normal reader to a *digital screen reader*. With high motivation, you will

- engage both sides of the brain;
- get the memory involved;
- use your tool kit to the maximum.

Turbo Speed

You took advantage of the relativistic nature of the brain when you trained with the metronome. We explained earlier that the brain allows you to "shift gears" into a higher level of efficiency and stay there continually. Let us illustrate what relativistic brain means with an example. You have driven on a highway at 75 miles per hour for one hour. When you exit the highway, it is difficult to slow down your speed to a lower limit of, for example, 35 miles per hour, because the brain is accustomed to going forward much faster.

You can now use the flexibility of the brain to shift comfortably into turbo-charged power and speed. Practice turbo technique with the text in Reading Exercise 5 on page 91.

Read the text and move your CS guide very fast, zipping along the lines so that you only notice the words. There is no need to "read" them; it is enough to imagine the text. Push yourself to do this faster and faster. Don't worry if your comprehension drops dramatically. Let it drop! Just look at the words and sentences, don't try to read them. Practice turbo for 5 minutes. Repeat 10 minutes every day for two weeks. After this exercise, you can return back to your "normal" reading speed. Due to the relativistic nature of the brain, you will notice that your speed will improve every day and that your comprehension will get better.

Relaxation Exercise E:
Whole Brain Breathing 4 x 4

Before the last reading exercise, you may relax with a technique that physically activates both sides of the brain. It is based on the maximum utilization of oxygen intake. If you feel the time span of counting to 4 too long, you may count to only 3 or even 2 and gradually increase the count up to 4.

1. With your left hand index finger, gently press the left nostril of your nose to close it. Exhale through your right nostril and count to 4 in your mind.

2. Before inhaling through your right nostril, count to 4.

3. Inhale through your right nostril and count to 4.

4. Release your left nostril, and with your right hand index finger, close your right nostril.

5. Count to 4 before exhaling through your left nostril.

6. Exhale through your left nostril and count to 4 in your mind.

7. Before inhaling through your left nostril, count to 4.

8. Inhale through your left nostril and count to 4.

9. Before exhaling, count to 4.

10. Repeat from point one.

Like the other relaxation exercises, this one can also be done in front of your computer monitor without bringing attention to yourself.

Reading Exercise 6: Combining all techniques. You have now formed a new habit—being a digital reader! Believe in your new habit, practice it every day, and be motivated enough to make this conscious change. If you have not yet made the decision, make it now. Use the relativistic nature of the brain and change to "turbo gear." Remember to do the following:

- Feel strong.
- Position yourself at an optimal distance from the screen.
- Find a comfortable position.
- Maintain a fast, steady beat.
- Imagine a picture on the topic before reading.
- Take more words at a time.
- Reduce fixation time.
- Stay on the page and concentrate.
- Use your guide.
- Move forward only.

Read the following text or go to the Web pages (www.hrdpress. com/effectivescreenreading/exercises.html) and calculate the number of words based on the 100-word dots in the left margin.

Pause—create an image in your mind of Broadway—and go.

Reading Exercise 6: Broadway

Broadway has been called the Street of Lights, the Great White Way. Actors, dancers and singers flock to Broadway from all over the world in pursuit of their dreams.

So what is this magical, mythical place? Broadway is actually a street running the length of Manhattan in New York City. But when people talk about "Broadway," they are usually referring to the section of Mid-town Manhattan which is dotted with theaters of the highest caliber in the world. Talented performers come to Broadway to complete for highly coveted roles in the shows.

- Playwrights dream of having their works performed on Broadway, it is the chance of a lifetime for most performing artists to be a part of "The Great White Way."

Many of the shows performed on Broadway are stage plays. But the shows that Broadway is known for are the musicals—spectacles of music, dance and acting which usually involve the most elaborate of sets. Much like the evolution of jazz music, this style of theatre, which developed into what is known today as a musical, is very much an American art form. And, also like
- jazz music, the origins of the American Musical are very deeply rooted in African American history and culture.

Dance and music have been a part of African-American culture since the days slaves were imported for plantation work. They brought with them the rhythms and traditions of their homelands in Africa and the Caribbean. From the start, slave owners were very interested in the black songs and dance. Before long, slave dances were used as a form of entertainment for the whites at social gatherings and formal balls. Thus, African dance and music became an important part of American culture. And in doing so, it made American styles of dance and music into performance, not just social entertainment. Without this influence, the birth of the American musical—theatrical performance integrating dance and music into the plot—would never have been possible.

Thanks to these beginnings, the all-American musical theatre made room for many black performers—unlike other performing arts which were primarily reserved for the whites. In the first decade of this century, many blacks enjoyed successful careers on Broadway. In that decade, an all-black musical, "In Dahomey," even opened on Broadway. But in 1910, after the African-American heavyweight boxer Jack Johnson beat the white heavyweight champion Jim Jeffries, anti-black riots broke out around New York City. Most black performers left Broadway for Performance venues in the black neighborhood of Harlem.

The 1920s saw the return of African-American influence in full force on the Broadway stage. The musical, "Shuffle Along," was very successful on Broadway for over a year. The show's very successful on Broadway for over a year. The show's popularity made stars of many of its performers. The show was very important in the development of musical theatre because it used non-traditional styles of music, including ragtime and other jazzy sounds taken from the popular music of the times. The show also included every popular
● dance step of the time. Many critics and theatre historians have said that "Shuffle Along" redefined musical theatre. Rather than displaying a lot of dancers in fancy costumes and songs in many different styles of music, in "Shuffle Along" the songs and dances were put together in a style which told the story of the production.

"Shuffle Along" was also a marker in African-American history because it made legitimate the idea of romantic love between African-Americans. For the first time on an American stage, two blacks kissed. The people who made the show were so nervous about the
● risk of showing affection between blacks that they planned the kiss to occur right before the curtain so they could make a quick getaway if the audience got angry.

The musical also brought about a big interest in black dancing as being acceptable social dancing for whites. "Colored dance studios" opened up all over New York City to teach white kids the moves of the black dances. The popularity of African-American dance led the way for many more black musicals on Broadway and opened a door of opportunity for black choreographers—the creators of the dances.

- "Shuffle Along" not only helped to create the theatre style we think of today as American musical theatre, but it also secured a place for African-American performers and black shows on Broadway—the Great White Way. Black faces darkened the Great White Way in such hit shows as "Porgy and Bess"; "Bubblin' Brown Sugar"; "Showboat"; and "Ain't Misbehavin'." These shows are some of the most popular and most successful ever to have appeared on the Broadway stage. All of these shows have had revivals in community, regional, and school theatres and some even saw a second trip to the Broadway stage.

- But these four shows, though perhaps the most influential black shows, were not the only successful black shows to appear on Broadway. In the 1970s, black theatre had great success. Two of the stand-out shows were "Dreamgirls"—a story based on the career of Diana Ross and the Supremes, and "The Wiz," a jazzed up version of "The Wizard of Oz." These two shows started a trend of using funky disco beats and dancing in musicals, and a movie version was even made of "The Wiz" featuring the young Michael Jackson.

The late Twentieth Century saw the creation of even more successful

• African-American musicals. "Sarafina!," "Black and Blue" and "Five Guys Named Moe" all hit Broadway and/or toured America. In addition, black dancers and choreographers made their mark on the history of musical theatre. Tap dancer Honi Coles won awards for his performance in the Broadway show, "My One and Only," and the tap dancer and choreographer Gregory Hines met success on Broadway in addition to launching a film career. In 1980 he appeared in a historical event, "Black Broadway," a tribute to the black Broadway musicals of the past. (Many other important black theatre talents assembled for this

• special show including: Honi Coles; Nell Carter; and many other African-Americans who helped to shape the entertainment industry.)

In 1996, a new type of black musical opened to rave reviews on Broadway. This show, called, "Bring in 'da NOISE, Bring in 'da FUNK," was a standout in the long line of African inspired musicals because this show tries to cross ethnic boundaries through the pulsating style of tap dance. The musical is subtitled "A Tap/Rap Discourse on the Power of the Beat." The show explored the history of the African-American by

• trying to find out what history really is. The plot and themes of the show unfold under the inspiration that history does not happen to race or cultures, but to people. And in doing so, it attempted to reach not just a black following or display a black culture, but share the stories of different African-American individuals, from the times of slavery to hip-hop.

Imagine that you have been given a ticket to the opening night of "Bring in 'da NOISE, Bring in 'da FUNK." You are about to join the hundreds of excited theatre goers about to share in a little

● piece of history. You put on your best outfit and go to the Ambassador Theatre in Mid-town Manhattan. The bright lights of the marquis above the front entrance announcing the grand opening are nearly blinding. You hand your ticket to an usher clad in a plush red jacket. You can smell a mixture of perfumes, chocolates and dusty theatre curtains. You can feel the excitement in the air as another usher directs you to your seat. You sit down on the velvet cushioned chair just as the lights dim and the musicians spring into action with the overture—the pre-performance music.

● The heavy, velvet curtain lifts and you are pulled into a world of dance, noise and funk for the next two hours. The nine dancers take you through epi- sodes in the lives of many different African-Americans. In the first scene you join the dancing slaves on Eight- eenth Century ships sailing toward America. It was on these ships that the art of tap dance began, and you can almost feel the life-pulse of those first slaves as you watch the dancers beat and drum. In another scene, you feel as though your own life is being wrenched

- away as you watch actor Baakari Wright dance away the last seconds of his life before the rope around his neck pulls the life out of him in the soul-touching routine, "Lynching Blues." In "The Whirligig Stomp," you are taken back in time to Harlem in the 1920's, where big bands and the high life were where it was at. And you can almost feel the dancers sweat as your heart beats with the hip-hop rhythms as the show returns you to the streets of modern day New York City where rap and street dance were born.

- To summarize, there was such a level of commitment in these shows that they took theatre to a new level. These, along with others of the shows mentioned in this article, were unrestrained in their creative energy. The creators and performers invested themselves in each performance and they brought about the one-of-a-kind experiences that make going to the theatre a special experience. These shows have helped to bring American theatre to a higher level of excellence by doing more than entertaining, by finding ways to touch souls. It is understandable, when sharing the experience of one of these
- shows, that the roots of what you are watching run deep—they run all the way back to ships full of enslaved men and women who only shared one language—the language of music and dance. (©bbc.co.uk)

Effective Screen Reading

Total number of words in 1 minute: _____

Please enter your result in the reading progression chart in Figure 2.23 at the end of Chapter 2 and subjectively estimate your understanding (Very well, Well, Sufficiently, or Little).

The Real Benefit

How do you benefit when you are capable of changing reading speeds from normal to very fast? You will gain *more time.* You will spend less time reading your screen and devote more time to productive work. Reading, as such, is not "real work"—this actually starts after reading. Digital speed reading gives you more time at your disposal. What you do with the extra time is, of course, up to you. You can allow more time for decision making, analysis, idea generation, business and personal development, planning, etc. Perhaps you will read more or you might take an extra vacation. The choice is yours.

From the graph below, you will note how many days, weeks, and months you will benefit from reading faster. To come up with your figure, you need to estimate the total time spent on your daily reading. Take the following reading material into consideration:

- newspapers (domestic, foreign)
- trade journals (IT, telecommunications, business, etc.)
- reports (sales, costs, personnel, etc.)
- books (text, business, electronic, etc.)
- e-mail
- the Internet (Web pages, competition, digital news, surfing, etc.)
- your company's intranet
- advertising material

How many hours do you spend reading? Your daily figure can be anywhere from 1 to 10 hours. Now check from the reading progression chart (Figure 2.23) what your speed was in Reading Exercise 0 (the reference point). Compare this to your achievements on the right (Reading Exercises 1 through 6). Have you at any point made an increase of 50 percent or even 100 percent? Have you doubled your speed? For example, if you started at 220 wpm and at some point reached 440 wpm or more, your increase is 100 percent (double). Have you tripled your speed? If you can maintain this velocity and comprehension with your everyday reading, you will have the extra time indicated in Figure 2.22 at your disposal. The total extra time available depends on the total hours you currently use for everyday reading. The more you read and the faster you become, the more time you will gain.

		Increase in Your Reading Speed		
		20%	50%	100% (2x)
Your Reading Time per Day (hours)	1	4 days	8 days	2.5 weeks
	2	8 days	3 weeks	5 weeks
	3	12 days	5 weeks	2 months
	4	16 days	6½ weeks	2½ months
	5	20 days	2 months	3 months
	6	24 days	2½ months	3½ months

Figure 2.22: Extra time available annually with the increase in reading speed (200 working days annually, 40 hours of work per week).

Summary and Onward

You have now added the main techniques of digital speed reading to your tool kit. The eye-brain system has been explained as well as how it can be utilized in an optimum manner to achieve maximum effectiveness in front of your computer screen. Before revealing how these techniques can be used with e-mail and the Internet, some advice will be offered on improving your concentration, understanding, and memorization when reading from computer screens.

	Reading Exercises							Self-Practice		
	0	1	2	3	4	5	6			
WPM	Ref.	+3S	Guide	Vision	Brain	PDS	Turbo	1 wk.	1 mo.	6 mo.
2,000										
1,800										
1,600										
1,400										
1,200										
900										
800										
700										
600										
500										
400										
300										
200										
100										
Understanding/Comprehension During Reading*										
V W										
W										
S										
L										

*Understanding During Reading Key:

VW = Very Well (over 75%)
W = Well (51–75%)
S = Sufficiently (25–50%)
L = Little (under 25%)

Figure 2.23: Reading progression chart.

— 3 —
Screen Reading Environment

The first part of Chapter 3 will offer additional techniques to achieve the maximum level of concentration essential for efficient screen reading. These techniques include improved motivation, correct use of breaks, positive attitude as well as using to the maximum all senses and skills on both sides of the brain. Needless to say, the environment has great impact on the degree of your concentration.

The second part of this chapter will deal with the topic of working environment. As the time spent in front of the display increases constantly, it is essential to look into proper lighting conditions. The contrast, resolution, and flickering of a computer screen all play an extremely important role. Recommendations for the right type of table, chair, monitor, mouse, and keyboard are presented. You will find practical advice on their positioning, space requirements, and a handful of tips for better body ergonomics. In addition, room temperature, atmosphere, as well as possible sounds and disturbances are discussed.

During the past decade, attention has been directed by office workers to the ergonomic factors that they encounter in their workplace. Some 20 to 30 years ago, work-related problems were caused mainly by employees doing too much heavy work. Today, these problems are mainly attributed to people doing too much light work, because the workforce is more and more engaged in the use of computers.

The ability to achieve peak personal performance in front of a computer depends on maintaining a high level of concentration all the time and enjoying what you are doing—the reading task. Only these will guarantee a profound understanding of the material you are reading and a satisfactory memory retention of the topics covered over a long period of time.

Your goals for a particular reading task will determine speed reading techniques and approaches applied. Vary these optimally, and you will be better able to manage the multitude of information offered by the Internet and e-mail. Furthermore, optimize your physical working environment with regards to lighting and ergonomics, maintain good quality hardware, and only use the very latest software versions.

Concentration

Efficient screen reading is the result of setting your mind completely into the text. Without concentration through relaxation, all other techniques will loose their value and have no significant impact on your digital reading speed. However, besides relaxation, there are some other factors that influence your capacity to maintain concentration on the subject matter.

Among others, these include your

- level of motivation;
- body's optimal performance time;
- spirit or mood in general;
- capability to benefit from all senses;
- ability to use both sides of the brain;
- breaks.

Motivation

The principal reason for poor motivation or lack of interest toward a reading task is often attributed to the lack of clearly defined reading goals. A clear strategy for extracting required information and remembering vital points must be kept in mind. Your motivation will be substantially increased with the following three-step fundamental approach:

Step 1: Vision—Why am I reading this text?

Step 2: Goal—What am I searching for in this text?

Step 3: Action—What will I do with the information?

Always set your vision and goals before starting to read. By pinpointing before hand what it is you are searching for, when you read the text, your mind will be actively looking for this information. This keeps your motivation and concentration high, and as a consequence, retrieval of key information will be much faster. Time will be saved and your efficiency improved. Keep the global picture in mind, and you will locate valuable pieces of information in minimum time and know instantly how to act on them.

Knowing Your Body

Learn to recognize your optimal time periods for maximum efficiency. These are the hours of the day when you are able to reach *your* peak personal performance. For example, it is not advisable to start with a demanding project after lunch when all the energy goes into digesting food. Ask yourself: "What time of the day am I most productive?" For many people, this is during the first two or three hours in the morning; for some it is late afternoon or even late evening. Observe your habits to find out your peak performance time, and perform your most demanding tasks during this time period.

Take advantage of every opportunity to stretch, change position, and walk around. Maintain relaxed shoulders, and keep your internal balance as low as possible. Raise your feet momentarily on the table to improve blood circulation.

The best ergonomics for your body is to alternate among several different types of tasks during the working day, since different assignments give the body an opportunity to recover while remaining productive. Throughout the day, it is recommended to have regular pauses, which do not have to be long—anything from 30 seconds up to a few minutes is sufficient. During these short breaks, you can perform simple exercises, like breathing deeply. All this will help your body eliminate the effects of boredom and fatigue.

In Chapter 2, we presented five easy and fast relaxation exercises, the purpose of which is to improve your concentration by freeing up your mind. Here are some additional tips to relax your body and eyes. These include massage, stretch, shrug, rotation, yawn, and blink. (You should refrain from doing any exercise that feels uncomfortable.)

- To reduce cramping/stiffness in your hands and fingers, gently massage them. Blood circulation is improved, and your hands will get warmer.

- To freshen up your whole upper body, do the "executive stretch." Clasp your hands behind your head and gently stretch your elbows back, taking in a deep breath as you stretch back.

- Do a shoulder shrug by raising up your shoulders toward your ears and then relax them downward. This will reduce tension and stiffness in the upper back and neck area.

- To improve blood circulation to your legs and feet, while seated, do some foot rotations. Rotate each ankle five times clockwise and five times counter-clockwise.

- Keep your eyes lubricated by yawning, blinking, and closing them.

- Relax the eye muscles by changing focus frequently. First look at your fingertips with your arm stretched in front of you. Then change focus by looking at a point far away from you. Now come back and look again at your fingertips. Repeat this at least three times.

Keep your head up and eyes looking forward most of the time. Your shoulders should be relaxed and hands in line with the forearms. Place the upper part of the monitor at eye height and minimum arm's distance away. Sit with your back erect and well supported. Have your feet firmly on the floor or on a footrest, and apply only moderate pressure at the front of the seat cushion. Keep the mouse close to your hand. Always have all other necessary material close by for easy reference.

Your eyes also need exercise. The accommodation capability—the ability of the eyes to change focus—gets weaker as you get older. The eye muscles become tired much faster and respond slower when focusing on the text. This natural weakening of the eyes, especially for people over 40, requires regular exercise. With proper training, it is possible to reduce the side effects. Dr. William Bates has investigated the topic in detail, and the results are presented in his book *Better Eyesight without Glasses* (1995).

Positivism

You should maintain a favorable attitude toward all your reading challenges. Talk to yourself in an inspiring manner and find positive aspects from the text. If you feel that you are in a non-inspiring mood, do your reading at a more convenient and productive time.

Senses and Whole-Brain Reading

Learn how to use your five senses to "tune up" yourself to the subject more efficiently. Combine your senses:

- **Vision (sight).** Look at the text and other elements on the screen and have a vision in mind regarding the purpose of the reading.

- **Auditory (hearing).** Listen to the sounds from the speakers, the rattle of the keyboard, and the clicking of the mouse.

- **Kinesthesia (touch).** Use all the input devices; feel the keyboard, desk, and CS guide in your hands, sense your body's position.

In your imagination, use smell and taste. Imagine that the topic you are reading has a favorite smell and "munch" it in your mouth. Benefit from the skills from both sides of your brain. By combining multisensory input with whole-brain reading, your motivation will be improved. Rhythm, movement, colors, overview, and imagination situated in the right hemisphere will all help you increase the level of concentration. The left hemisphere needs no special attention; it will automatically be involved. Make sure that all your reading tasks become pleasurable moments that you thoroughly enjoy.

Breaks

The amount of breaks you take from reading on-screen and what you do during them affect your comprehension and ability to focus. Computer work requires frequent breaks. Due to various factors, reading from the screen for many hours a day is extremely demanding for the eyes, brain, and body. Rather than keeping to a 15-minute break every 2 hours, it is recommended that you keep a

1-minute pause every 15 to 20 minutes, and a 5 to 10 minute pause every hour.

Studies on the human memory (Russell 1994) clearly demonstrate that people remember more in the beginning and at the end of a reading task. This phenomenon is called the *Von Restorff effect* (see Figures 3.1 and 3.2*)*. The memory is the highest in the beginning and at the end of a 1-hour reading task. The middle parts are more difficult to remember, and the memory level normally stays below 50 percent. Multiple breaks in a 1-hour reading task will contribute in adding more beginnings and endings to the reading, both of which will improve the memory and accelerate learning. The middle parts are no longer so difficult to remember, and you are able to maintain memory levels over 50 percent during almost all of the reading task.

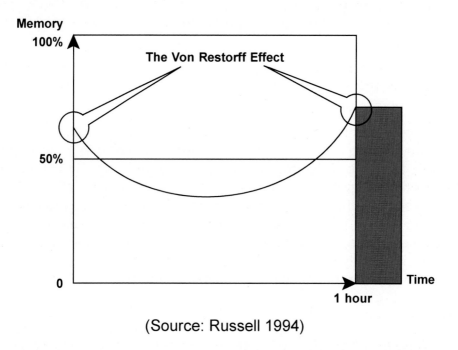

(Source: Russell 1994)

Figure 3.1: The Von Restorff effect with one break (the gray bar).

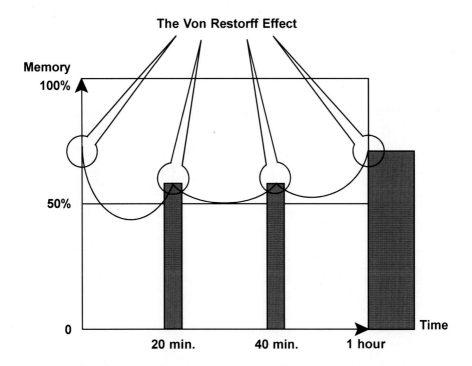

Figure 3.2: The Von Restorff effect with multiple breaks.

The area highlighted in Figure 3.3 represents the increase in memory during a 1-hour reading with two breaks compared to only one break in the end.

Understanding

In Chapter 1, we briefly dealt with the versatile subject of under-standing (comprehension). Some generally accepted ideas on what happens to comprehension when the reading speed increases were mentioned. Most people maintain the idea that in order to understand a text very well, it must be read slowly and carefully. Consequently, the faster we read, the less we would understand.

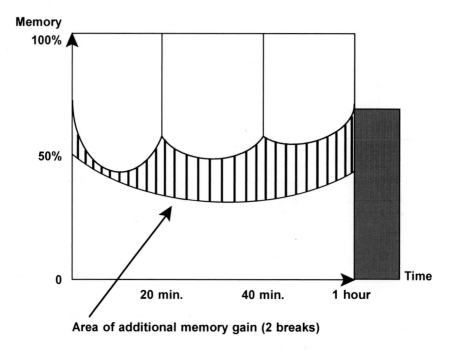

Figure 3.3: The Von Restorff effect with multiple breaks and the memory benefit.

Imagine how many words there are in your head. Each one has its own special associations, feelings, thoughts, sensory input, connections, and memories. These associations are only yours. During reading, your interpretation of an individual word may not be the same as the author's. With an increase in your reading speed, you are less likely to stray from the author's intent. As the brain has very little time to make "unnecessary" associations, you don't get stuck anymore with individual words. You can visualize the overall picture much easier and understand the key messages.

To summarize, reading speeds below 200 wpm actually make your understanding worse. You need to maintain a speed *high enough* for good comprehension—a range of 450 to 900 wpm (see Figure 3.4). Of course, exceeding your current reading capacity too much and too soon will result in a deterioration in your understanding. For the majority of people, this deterioration occurs after 1,000 wpm, even though there are exceptions to this main rule. Your present capacity can, of course, be increased with practice.

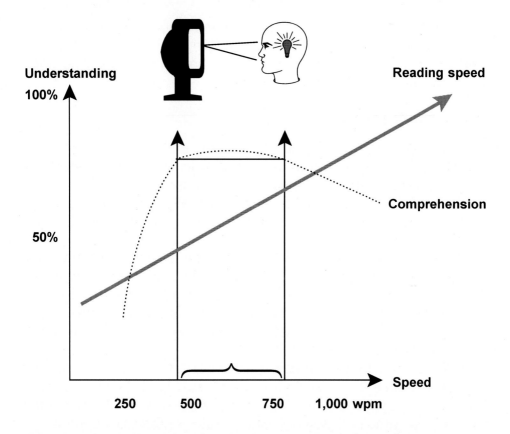

Figure 3.4: Correlation of reading speed and understanding. To maintain good understanding (60 to 80%), a speed high enough (450–900 wpm) is needed.

There is no sense in reading a text if your understanding drops to a very low level. There are various reasons why your comprehension level may be low: your vocabulary may be deficient and consequently affects your understanding; the material may be confusing; the techniques for screen reading may feel awkward to you; using screen reading techniques distracts you from the text itself; there are outside disturbances, interferences, etc. Your comprehension might also be affected if you do not have the overall picture in mind. Here the technique of Applied Imagination (see Chapter 2) will be useful.

You should get yourself actively involved and make notes during reading or immediately after finishing the task. A powerful method for note taking and memory enhancement is called Mind Mapping developed by Tony Buzan.

Screen Mind Mapping

A Mind Map® or Mind Mapping® is a powerful graphical technique that harnesses the full range of cortical skills from both sides of the brain. Applying Mind Mapping to the computer screen is called *Screen Mind Mapping*, which uses specially designed software. Nowadays there are various types of programs available for easy Mind Mapping on the screen.

Mind Mapping provides a universal key to unlock the potential of the brain in a single, uniquely powerful way. Mind Maps will improve learning and assist in clearer thinking to achieve maximum performance. This technique will bring order and logic to the chaos that often prevails in the head. It helps clarify the mind when thoughts seem to be jumbled.

With a Mind Map, you can quickly get an overview of a broad subject, because it allows you to gather and hold vast amounts of data on a single sheet of paper or a screen shot. A Mind Map encourages problem solving and idea generation, because it enables you to see logical and new creative pathways. The technique can be used in making both written and verbal communication more precise in order to present key messages clearer and reach desired goals faster. In businesses, it has been used in planning, creating visions, managing projects, and formulating general strategy as well as in managing people and meetings more efficiently.

A Mind Map can be made by hand or by computer software. The instructions on how to make it are as follows:

1. Start in the center with an image, a symbol, or a key word of the topic.

2. Use images, symbols, codes, and dimension.

3. Select key words and print with capital letters.

4. Each word or image should be alone on its own line.

5. The lines are connected starting from the central image. The central lines are thicker, organic, and flowing, becoming thinner as they radiate from the center.

6. The lines are about the same length as the word/image.

7. Use your own color code throughout the Mind Map.

8. Develop your own personal style.

9. Use emphasis and show associations.

10. Keep the Mind Map clear by using hierarchy, numerical order, or outlines to embrace the branches.

Throughout this book, we have used a program called Mind-Manager, although various other software programs are commercially available for a Mind Map presentation.

A Mind Map

- attracts the eye-brain system;
- contains only key words;
- shows clearly the links and connections;
- is enjoyable to look at, read, and muse over.

The impact on the memory is extremely positive.

Long-Term Memory

Because human memory, unfortunately, works through forgetting, how can we remember important new information for a long period of time? The only way to recall subject matter on a long-term basis is through a series of orderly repetitions after the learning period.

Using the Mind Mapping technique can help you learn information over the long term. A Mind Map is typically condensed to a format that fits on a single sheet of paper or on your screen and can be reviewed in just a few minutes. Sufficient and orderly repetitions will insert the topic and its contents in the permanent (long-term) memory. The repetitions should follow an orderly sequence (see Figure 3.5) after the learning period. Naturally, the time needed for each repetition will depend on the amount of information contained in the Mind Map or other summary.

Repetition Number	Time After Learning	Duration of Repetition
1	10 minutes	5 – 10 minutes
2	1 day	5 minutes
3	1 week	5 minutes
4	1 month	5 – 10 minutes
5	6 months	5 minutes
Total time needed for repetitions:		25 – 35 minutes

Figure 3.5: The rules of repetition for long-term memory.

Ergonomics

The content of labor has drastically changed during the past 30 years. Hard physical work is becoming rare as factories become more and more automated, and strenuous tasks are shifted to robots. Increasing numbers of employees work for the service sector and primarily manage information. Work-related studies (for example Finnish Institute for Occupational Health, 2004) have revealed that over 60 percent of office employees suffer from repetitive stress or stress-related injuries. These include aching, numbing, tingling, or unspecified pain in the neck and back area, cramped shoulders, and sore wrists, hands, and fingers. Four main factors can be found:

1. Incorrect work habits
2. Continuous use of a computer mouse
3. Long periods of repetitive, monotonous motion
4. Improper work environment

The computer work environment receives more attention as the number of injuries increases at an alarming rate. Diseases directly attributed to working with computers such as carpal tunnel syndrome (CTS), tendonitis, De Quervain´s tendonitis, and tenosynovitis mean high costs both for the employer and for society, when surgical treatments, hospitalization, medication, absences, retraining, and possibly even early retirements are necessary. For example CTS, which is a chronic inflammation in the wrist area, can be caused by continuous work with the mouse. It often compels the patient to start using the mouse permanently with the other hand. Workers also suffer from other problems such as headaches, eye irritation, fatigue, poor concentration, and stress, the causes of which are sometimes difficult to trace. Much of this discomfort can be avoided with proper ergonomics in the workplace, as these symptoms are often the result of pushing the body beyond its natural limits.

Ergonomics is the science of studying the work environment. The goal is to find optimal working conditions and prevent work-related diseases. Ergonomics focuses on proper lighting and suitable equipment such as desk, chair, display, keyboard, and mouse. Other factors studied include temperature, atmosphere, and possible disturbances.

Lighting

Three factors play key roles when determining correct lighting conditions at your workplace. These are background lighting, screen contrast and its resolution, as well as flickering of your computer monitor.

Background Lighting

The main challenges with lighting are related to the positioning of the light sources and the general level of the light. When working with a computer, it is recommended that the general level of the light in the area should be dimmer than when working with printed matter. Since we normally need both computer and paper, you should select a relatively dim room or background lighting, with an adjustable reading lamp for printed matter. The lamps must be angled away from the eyes and monitor. If light sources are positioned incorrectly, they will

- cause reflections on the screen;
- contribute in slowing down the reading speed;
- cause eye irritation.

Lamps positioned in front of you are often in the field of vision, and lamps behind you often cause glare on the screen. This limits the position of lamps only to either side. If the display faces a window, the outside light may cause disturbing glare. Reflections may also be due to clothing, walls, table, surfaces, and other tools. See Figure 3.6, which illustrates ergonomics and lighting.

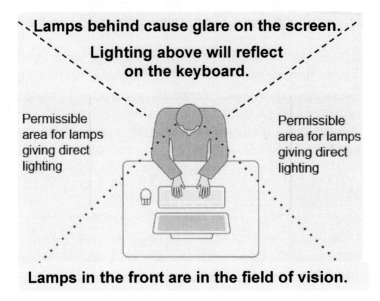

Lamps behind cause glare on the screen.
Lighting above will reflect on the keyboard.

Permissible area for lamps giving direct lighting

Permissible area for lamps giving direct lighting

Lamps in the front are in the field of vision.

Figure 3.6: Ergonomics and lighting.

Ask the following key questions regarding lighting:

1. What am I doing and what are the tools needed to accomplish it?
2. What kind of light source is the best?
3. What is the optimum angle of light?

The solution to the first question is simply to eliminate all unnecessary material from the vicinity of the computer display. What is not needed should not be at the worktable. Reflective materials such as glass, desk pads, framed photographs, statues, souvenirs, diplomas, and any other similar objects should be removed from the immediate proximity of the monitor to avoid distracting reflections. Many people tend to collect these items on their work desk because they usually have some emotional attachment to them. However, these items should be placed somewhere other than close to the screen.

Questions 2 and 3 relate to the type of light and the angle at which the light comes to the room. The recommendations are pretty standard: use indirect light for overall lighting and table lamps for direct lighting. All lamps should emit clear, even, and soft light. To avoid glare and reflections, the source of light (i.e., the light bulb) should not be visible.

For overall room lighting, indirect lighting is recommended, because it allows the light beams to enter the room from the ceiling or from a reflecting surface located above the light source. This provides a much softer light.

Alternatively, direct lighting (table lamps) may be used if placed on either side of the display, as explained earlier. This will, however, decrease the flexibility of the arrangement of the workstation.

If your workplace does not have indirect lighting, you may try to remove some light bulbs or change their direction. Reflections can be discovered by holding a mirror in front of the display and observing if any actual light sources can be noticed in the mirror. Display reflection shields are also available, but they tend to make doing work at the computer difficult. Of course, the best solution is achieved with fixtures designed specifically to give indirect lighting.

The Computer Screen and Natural Light

Natural light is not always ideal for computer work. It can be uneven and create unnecessary glare on your monitor, increasing eyestrain. If you work close to a window, take these factors into consideration.

First, the monitor should not be positioned directly facing the window. The outside light will cause a strong glare on the screen, which will greatly strain the eyes. The same happens if the monitor is positioned parallel to the window. The outside glare will come directly to the eyes and may create a sharp contrast with the screen, causing excessive fatigue.

One alternative is to turn the display to face the window *diagonally* or *sideways*. However, if the sun outside is very bright, even this might not reduce the glare. The solution is to use curtains, shades, or some kind of blinds. On the other hand, natural light and occasional glances outside will greatly stimulate the mind and give the eyes needed regular exercise. It is advisable to experiment with various combinations of natural and artificial light. The objective is to achieve lighting conditions that make reading from the screen most efficient.

Screen Contrast and Resolution

Properly adjusting the screen contrast will help reduce eyestrain and fatigue. The goal is to achieve the greatest possible text clarity on the screen. The *contrast* is defined as the difference between the text and its background—the intensity relationship between the brightest and darkest pixels. Today's display technology offers ratios from 100:1 to as high as 300:1. The user-adjustable parameters for the backlighting can normally be found on the front of the monitor. They include brightness, dimness, and color (just like on a TV). Don't be satisfied with the factory presetting; try different combinations to find out what pleases *your* eyes most.

A good contrast in the text will increase reading speed, understanding, and overall efficiency. The text on the screen will open up new possibilities, since the optimal contrast can be achieved using colors. Everyone has their own preferences with color combinations for print and background that are attractive and appeal to the eyes. Here again the rule of thumb is to use high-contrast, natural screen colors. Typical favorites include the following:

- black or blue print on white background
- white on black
- black on light blue
- dark blue on yellow

Since lighting conditions may vary during the day, there is no one-time setting. Vary the screen contrast to compensate for the changes in lighting conditions, and find the settings that match your personal taste.

Effective Screen Reading

Flickering

One important factor affecting the picture quality is the *refresh rate*. Refresh rate (or refresh frequency) means how many times the display card unit updates the picture on the screen in one second. The light has a frequency of 50 Hz (Hertz)—it "flickers" about 50 times per second. The picture on the screen should therefore flicker (or be updated) at least 50 times per second in order to minimize eyestrain. A good quality graphics display adapter card increases the refresh rate of the screen over 50 Hz. This is good for the eyes, because it exceeds the frequency of the light. Most of the displays sold today have refresh rates between 50 and 120 Hz—the picture is drawn on the screen 50 to 120 times each second. Higher refresh rates mean better ergonomics and, consequently, less fatigue for the eyes.

If your monitor is below 50 Hz, you will experience uncomfortable flickering of the screen, and your eyes will get tired very fast. This is especially noticeable in an open office environment where the flickering of a neighbor's display may disturb the reading efficiency of others. In Chapter 2, we explained that your peripheral vision allows you to see rapid movements in the environment unconsciously. This characteristic may cause your concentration to deteriorate. To compensate for this problem, you can always use some type of movable screen, posters, or even cardboard to isolate your work station from distractions.

Equipment

The equipment involved in computer screen reading includes worktable, chair, display, keyboard, and mouse. These should be of good quality. They represent visually the value of your thoughts and reinforce your mind positively or negatively through sense and touch. Before purchasing any new office furniture, it is advisable to personally go and test it at the store.

Table

You should have enough space on the main working surface. People are often taken by surprise by how much space the computer display actually occupies on the worktable. Working levels, shelves, and other furniture should be organized in such a manner that the working position remains comfortable and the work flow is flexible. The height of the table should be adjustable, and it should offer the possibility to incorporate new sub-levels.

In work requiring constant use of a mouse, you should use a worktable with an opening for the stomach. The sides of the table will support the arms because the chair, in this case, will have no armrests.

Working Zones

You can easily organize your work area for a more comfortable and efficient performance. The area in question comprises a work desk, sub-levels, and shelves. An ergonomic use of a computer dictates that the area under the desk be kept clear of cables and other material to allow sitting without getting twisted up. This also applies to cords connecting the keyboard and mouse, although the tendency is toward cordless input devices.

The actual work area can be divided into three zones:

1. The *hot* zone. This is the area at your fingertips. Keep most-used items including keyboard and mouse in this area.

2. The *neutral* zone. This is within arm's reach and where often-used items such as telephone, tape, stapler, etc., are located.

3. The *reference* zone. This lies beyond arm's reach and you have to get up to collect items kept in this area. Keep materials such as files, reference books, telephone books, printers, etc., in this area.

See Figure 3.7, which illustrates these three zones.

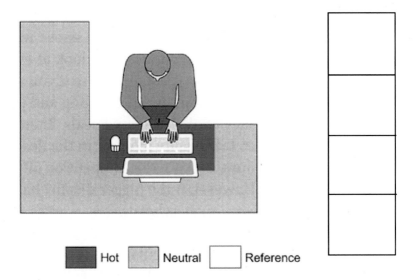

Figure 3.7: Zones of your work area.

Place books and other reference materials between knee and shoulder height on shelves for easy access. Avoid reaching and twisting when you lift items from shelves.

Chair

Sit comfortably at the back of the chair and keep your feet firmly on the floor. This is ergonomically the right position and will reduce fatigue in the body. Make sure that the edge of the chair does not press into the backs of your knees or thighs and that both your feet are well supported, either on the floor or on a footrest. A foot or leg support is recommended if you need to raise the chair to keep your wrists straight.

The chair must be flexible and allow as many working positions as possible. It should provide support for the legs, arms, and back. The height of the armrests must be adjustable. This will eliminate the need to hunch shoulders or slouch down in the chair in order to use the armrests comfortably. The backrest must support the hip and the lower back. The seat back should be adjustable to support the most curved part of the back. Sometimes a pillow might be necessary. The other alternative is to use a variety of stools without a backrest. Try to sit with your elbows close to the body, relax your shoulders, keep your wrists straight, and have forearms supported more or less horizontally. Remember to keep the head straight. Move from the hip joints.

The Computer Screen

On a long-term basis, the most important tool for the screen reader is the computer screen. It is strenuous to look at even a good-quality monitor for several hours a day; it is even worse if you are using a poor one. In this respect, take great care when selecting and purchasing your computer, and be especially wary of package deals. There is a great tendency to include a low-cost, low-quality monitor in the deal when the price is being cut to the minimum. Check if the competition offers a larger monitor for the same price. However, if the bigger display has poor image quality, it can cause problems such as headaches, eyestrain, and other stress injuries.

Whatever monitor you buy, remember to keep the screen clean by wiping off the dust and fingerprints regularly.

Positioning the monitor. The top of the monitor should be positioned below eye level, in much the same way as a book you are reading. If your worktable consists of two independently adjustable parts, lower the part where the monitor sits to create a viewing angle of 25 degrees or more.

If your monitor is positioned on top of the central processing unit, change your installation. Looking at a screen that is positioned on top of the central processing unit reduces the number of times the eyes blink, which results in the eyes drying, because your tear ducts release fewer teardrops. This is the main reason why the monitor should ideally be positioned below horizontal eye level.

As explained earlier, the distance to the screen from your eyes should be anywhere from 2 feet all the way up to 2½ to 3 feet.

The optimum distance to the computer screen will be determined by the following:

1. The legibility of the monitor:

    - brightness (contrast, lucidity, uniformity)
    - size and sharpness (focus, convergence)
    - clarity, geometry, and purity of colors

2. The amount of text, its size, font type, and positioning on the screen

3. The surrounding lighting conditions (direct light, indirect light)

4. The quality of the monitor, especially its refresh rate

5. Reader's vision capability, i.e., good "screen sight":

   - Sharpness of vision: the ability to focus eyes sharply on the text and to see pictures clearly

   - Sufficient field of vision: the ability to capture the whole screen with one glance and to make detailed observations even from the margins of a larger screen

   - Vision for contrast and dim light: the ability to see shades of gray

   - Tolerance for glare: the ability to compensate flickering of the screen or sudden reflections of light from the screen

   - Dynamic vision for depth: the ability to compensate variable reading distances during the workday

Remember that the reading distance to the screen should be *double* that to a book. See Figure 3.8, which illustrates the correct distance and viewing angle to a monitor.

Display technologies. Various types of display technologies are available today and the development is very rapid. Cathode ray tube (CRT) technology has traditionally been used for computer screens and has maintained its leadership for decades. The picture quality/price-relation of CRT technology has traditionally been the highest.

All new monitors have refresh rates over 50 Hz. A standard for the industry averages 75 to 80 Hz and some manufacturers go well over 100 Hz. Flat screens represent another form of CRT technology with refresh rates horizontally up to 100 Hz and vertically up to 160 Hz. These displays are also called ThinCRT or FED displays (field emission display).

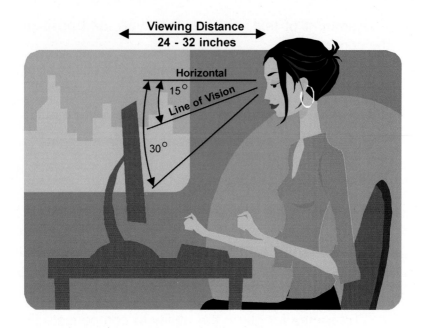

Figure 3.8: The correct distance and viewing angle to a monitor.

The challenger for CRTs has come from screens based on liquid crystal display (LCD) technology. These thin displays do not flicker, and the monitor occupies much less valuable space on the worktable. In addition, a smaller 15-inch LCD is equivalent to a larger 17-inch CRT screen, when the actual, usable display area is measured. Proper reading distance for a 15-inch LCD is 2 to 2½ feet and for a 13-inch, about 20 inches.

Other technologies—besides CRT and LCD—include, among others, Electroluminescent, Ferroelectric LCD, Light Emitting Polymer (LEP), Organic Light Emitting Display (OLED) and Thin Film Transistor.

Even the best CRT or LCD displays achieve a resolution of a little over 100 pixels per inch. Intensive research is being done by major computer manufacturers to double this resolution. Prototypes already utilize 2,560 x 2,048 pixels in a 16-inch screen, which means roughly 200 pixels per inch. There is a definitive advantage: smaller pixels improve the quality of the text. The curves of the letters and all thin lines will have a more refined display and the readability will improve greatly. New applications are available as drawings, maps, and medical images can now be sent electronically and displayed at the receiving end with excellent accuracy.

Keyboard and Mouse

The main input devices to a computer are the keyboard and the mouse. Since these are the items used most frequently, their handling should be made as comfortable as possible. Other input devices include CD-Rom and different types of joysticks. Both the keyboard and the mouse can be positioned at the same or lower level as your work desk. Make sure that your hands and wrists are supported by the work level or by the armrests of your chair in order to maintain a straight wrist position.

Keyboard. To achieve the right typing position, let your arms drop naturally to your sides with elbows at 90-degree angles. When placing your hands above the keyboard, you should extend them straight from the forearm and keep your wrists straight. The fingers can be curled slightly. Depending on the chair and especially when using a mouse, it is much more comfortable to have your forearms supported.

Various types of keyboards are available on the market. With a good keyboard, the keys need only a light, gentle touch, but are still stiff enough to avoid accidental double clicking. When you press the keys, the sound is low, and the keys remain steady at their position without extra movements to any side. A good keyboard is designed so that typing feels natural. All characters should be found at standard places without the need to search for them individually.

As an alternative to a standard keyboard, you can use a "natural" or ergonomic keyboard. It may prove especially useful if you have to type a lot. A "natural keyboard" is bent in the middle to form a boomerang shape, allowing your hands to remain in a normal position. The result is less tension in the shoulder area. However, a natural keyboard requires a little more space on your table, and the position of the mouse is farther away. With some keyboards, it is possible to adjust the sound of individual keys to be *on* or *off*. If you want to dampen the keyboard sound, place an extra mouse pad under it. Typing many hours a day can be a very tiresome task, and to break the tedium and monotony you may want to experiment by frequently alternating between the keyboard and other input devices such as the mouse.

Mouse. Various types of mice are available on the market. Be sure to get a high-quality one. You can be assured that by paying a little extra, it will re-pay you many times over. Consider the following when buying a mouse:

- how it fits into your hand
- how it feels
- how the buttons work

The mouse is used more and more, and consequently, its performance plays a key role. It should be large enough in order for your hand to rest conveniently on top of it and your fingers lie naturally on the buttons. The clicking sound of some mice can be too loud or the buttons may feel too stiff. However, if the buttons are too sensitive, it may result in troublesome and erroneous clicks. The movement must be light and consistent. One of the most irritating things is an unpredictable and unreliable mouse.

As stated earlier, prolonged, improper use of a low-quality mouse can result in a very difficult and painful stress injury such as carpal tunnel syndrome. The cure for this disease is sometimes simply changing the mouse from one hand to the other. To avoid mouse-related stress injuries, use your (high-quality) mouse in a proper way to achieve greater comfort and ergonomics.

The same working principles are applicable with a mouse as with a keyboard. Make your upper arms drop naturally to your sides without shrugging your shoulders. You may need to raise the chair or lower the table. Let your right or left hand rest gently on the mouse, having your forearm supported. Make sure that your wrist and palm are also supported by the table. Avoid resting them on the edge of a desk. Take advantage of an extra palm/wrist support that will considerably reduce the stress on your wrist. A proper wrist support is essential when using the mouse throughout the day. Perhaps the best supports are those that are filled with gel, because their shape will follow the anatomy of your wrist.

Try to minimize clicking and dragging. If these tasks are necessary, use only a light touch to click and drag. Take extra time to thoroughly learn the user's manual of the mouse. This will often help you become more efficient at using your computer and eliminate unnecessary clicking and dragging. Take advantage of the keyboard shortcuts for the most often-used commands, to greatly reduce the need for clicking the mouse. Many times these commands are actually the same in different programs. For example, most programs running under Windows can be operated completely without the mouse. Saving a document in the middle of typing takes place much faster from the keyboard (Ctrl S) than unnecessarily moving and clicking the mouse.

Keep the mouse as close as possible to the keyboard to minimize any unnecessary reaching from the shoulder. The mouse itself should be moved only in a very small area. You can enhance the performance of the mouse by changing its adjustments. Increasing the speed of the pointer will result in less movement on the mouse pad. A table-attachable mouse support can also be placed on top of the number block. This reduces turning the wrist to the side. Recent ergonomic studies have shown that a wrist angle over 15 degrees can cause movement and strain in the shoulder blade.

Another good habit is to alternate the hands when using the mouse. Using your left hand allows you to place it immediately next to the text keys. On the right side, you have to "jump over" two additional key blocks, forcing you to stretch your wrist more than 6 inches extra. When the mouse plays a more important role than the keyboard, place it in front of you and set the keyboard a little to one side.

It is advisable to test different models to find the most suitable mouse for your hand. Even individual mice in the same model group can have a great variation in stiffness and sensibility of movement. If your hand has a tendency to become cold, furnish the mouse with a cover or wear gloves with open fingertips.

Double clicking is very strenuous for the hand and fingers, because it is an unnatural function. Go to the Control Panel to adjust double clicking to be slow or change it to be a single click. In a three-button mouse, you can use the middle button to represent a double click. Alternatively, the middle button may be used to scroll down Web pages. You may, of course, vary its function during the workday.

Improved ergonomics include the "joystick" and trackball types of mice. In some models, the trackball under the mouse has been replaced with an optical recognition device, which eliminates the use of a mouse pad. The unit will work on any surface. Also a so-called "force feedback" mouse that increases speed and accuracy is already available on the market. This input device will mechanically give feedback to the user who will actually feel when the pointer finds the corner or the scroll bar, because there is a change in the resistance. A cordless mouse offers more flexibility in positioning and moving the unit.

A simple solution to achieve a neutral position and greater comfort while working with a mouse is to attach the unit into a "trapper." This is a mechanical, cursor-controlled unit to alternate between keyboard and traditional mouse without moving hands. It is designed to prevent work-related injuries for those who work with computers and use a mouse for extended periods. A trapper offers an ergonomically correct working position with arms centered against the body.

The unit moves the cursor with precision and accuracy and is equipped with the right and left clicking functions. A rubber-coated, balanced steel rod affects the mouse's control ball and provides cursor control. Click functions are transferred to the two keys, centrally located in front of the keyboard. The mouse can also be lifted out of its holder and used in a traditional manner. This allows other muscle groups to be used, which is good for the body.

Space

The space has a tremendous impact on the reading ability as a whole. Space as a general term means

- air and temperature of the room;
- general atmosphere of the ambiance;
- background sounds.

Air and Temperature

The air should be circulated so that the fresh outside air can enter the workspace. However, avoid a draft from open windows. If windows can't be opened, adjust the air conditioning to circulate new air into the room.

Although the most comfortable working temperature for a workspace is a matter of individual choice, the brain works best when the air temperature is constant and even a little on the cool side. Ideally this is between 64 and 68 degrees Fahrenheit. If you feel cold at this temperature, put on another layer of clothing. For the highest reading efficiency, make sure that the proper environmental conditions exist to keep your brain sharp.

Atmosphere

The reading area should be made comfortable and inviting. The atmosphere will greatly affect your performance, i.e., your overall screen reading efficiency. The atmosphere should be welcoming and pleasing to create the right tone for working.

Factors such as:

- sufficient lighting
- spacious ambiance
- color-coordinated decorations to please the eye
- well-organized work desk without clutter

all have a significant impact on your achievements. The area must invoke an inviting feeling, making you want to sit at the computer and start working.

Sounds and Disturbances

Background sounds such as music and outside disturbances greatly affect your ability to concentrate. Using background music is an individual choice—some like it, some find it distracting. Music increases the segregation of endorphin, a hormone related to the feeling of satisfaction. If music is used, the best type is instrumental with a beat of 60 to 80 pulses per second. The rhythm of the music should inspire the brain to relax and get the right hemisphere of the brain involved in the reading process (see Chapter 2).

Pay attention to the noise level of the computer, especially its central processing unit. Humming and whistling continuing for hours can get on anybody's nerves and lower their ability to concentrate. Even though you can become accustomed to the sound of the computer and not notice it anymore, the effects are felt at the sub-conscious level. This can become especially critical in an otherwise silent environment, when sounds are more easily heard. All computers and other equipment making distracting sounds should be placed as far as possible from the work desk. The central processing unit makes less sound if it is placed in a frame under the work-table. Computers specifically designed to be silent are also available on the market. People who are easily distracted by noise should invest a little more and buy a computer with a lower noise level.

Summary and Onward

Various environmental factors that influence computer screen reading efficiency have been explained. The correct conditions of lighting and a quality monitor positioned correctly on the worktable play a key role. Great care should be taken when selecting furniture and computer hardware. Ergonomic accessories such as wrist pads and mouse trappers should be used as well as shortcut keyboard commands to reduce unnatural movements of the wrist. The work space should be designed in such a manner that the atmosphere is inviting for any screen reading task. A sufficient amount of fresh air circulated with a temperature between 64 and 68 degrees will optimally stimulate the brain. Distracting noises must be eliminated or reduced to a minimum.

The next chapter of this book covers various aspects of e-mail that are a source of frustration and stress in many offices. We will illustrate how to apply ABCT^2 analysis to prevent e-mails from cluttering your inbox and wasting your valuable time.

— 4 —

Manage Your Daily E-mail

The surge of electronic mail (e-mail) during the past five years has been outstanding. It has been estimated by the Gartner Group that, in large companies, employees spend around three hours each day reading and writing e-mails. They all need efficient techniques to manage their e-mail system. Proper use of this communication tool is the key to effective work practice. Using e-mail etiquette to show respect for others will also project the right personal and company image. Companies need to establish and introduce principles for sending, receiving, and filing e-mails to their personnel.

In this section, we will provide some straightforward steps to manage your e-mail system and give advice on how to write good e-mails. You will learn how to use ABCT² analysis for both printed matter and e-mail for better time and self-management. This technique will help you prioritize your incoming mail and identify key messages much faster. You will also learn how to apply speed-reading techniques to the ever-growing pile of long e-mails.

E-mail Today

America Online, a leading company in telecommunications, did a study on the importance of e-mail and the Internet in 2001. At that time, almost 50 percent of the people interviewed said that the Internet had become a "necessity" in their lives. Given a preference, almost 70 percent of them said they would take an Internet connection, rather than TV or phone, while over 50 percent considered e-mail as the primary tool for communication in their daily business. In addition, many users felt totally dependent on e-mail as their daily tool for communication.

The importance of e-mail is best evidenced by its growth. In 1998, the number of e-mail addresses was, according to Messaging Online Research Center, about 280 million. Two years later, the same figure had grown to 570 million, and by 2002, there were more than 900 million addresses. In 2006, the estimation was at 1.2 billion, i.e., nearly one in five people on the planet were estimated to have their own e-mail address. How many addresses there will be by 2010 remains to be seen. See Figure 4.1, which illustrates the increase in e-mail addresses.

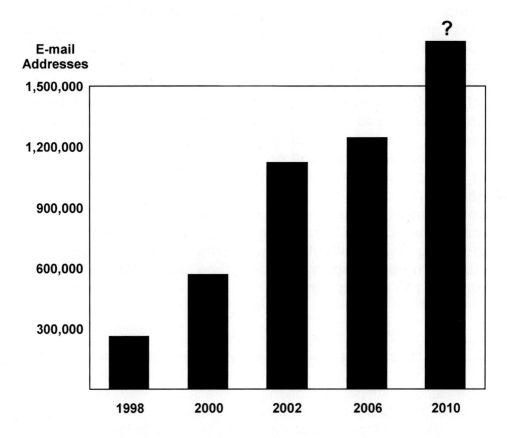

(Source: Messaging Online Research Center)

Figure 4.1: The number of e-mail addresses in the world from 1998 to 2010.

Effective Screen Reading

The main reasons for this tremendous growth can mainly be attributed to the following:

- ease, speed, and minimal expense of communication
- increase in Web services
- development of wireless communication
- shift away from fixed workplaces to mobile offices

The surge in Web services has meant that Web mail (using e-mail with a browser) accounts for more than half of all the different mail types (UNIX, POP, office systems such as MS Exchange, Lotus Notes, etc.). IDC—a subsidiary of IDG, a technology, media, research, and events company—estimates that this year—almost 97 billion e-mails will be sent every day through the global Internet computer network. What is alarming is that this will be the first year that the volume of trash mail (spam) is expected to exceed person-to-person e-mail volumes sent worldwide. Therefore, there is an urgent need for effective management of e-mail, both on the individual and corporate levels.

Having established that the management of e-mail flow is essential, the way in which e-mails are written is just as important. In this digital age, most of us have not written a letter for years since most business and private correspondence is done almost exclusively by e-mail. In today's business world, it can actually be crucial for permanent evidence to be kept of an e-mail sent or received.

The advantages of e-mail are evident. That said, we have all experienced our inboxes full of irrelevant and spurious e-mails containing jokes, special offers, discounts on products, links to various sites, etc. IDC estimates that in the next few years, messages like this will increase by over 40 times and the amount of money spent on e-mail advertising will surge from $164 million in 2000 to $7.3 billion in 2007. Nevertheless, close to 90 percent of businesspeople consider e-mail to be the number one communication tool.

We also need to look at common mistakes and misuse when sending e-mails. The most common e-mail "sins" committed was the subject of a European study commissioned by palmOne (2005). A sample group of 750 workers employed by large companies in various European countries was interviewed. The results were alarming.

First, the study revealed seven clear categories:

1. **Ignoring.** There is a clear tendency not to reply to many e-mails.

2. **Denying.** When asked, people pretend they never received a particular message.

3. **Making assumptions.** Sending an e-mail does not mean that it will be read.

4. **Wordiness.** There is a clear tendency to write more than necessary.

5. **All-inclusiveness.** E-mails are sent to everyone in the organization, even to those who are not concerned with the information and clearly do not require it.

6. **Sloppiness.** Messages are full of grammatical and spelling errors.

7. **Tactlessness.** Writers of e-mails use inappropriate tone.

Second, over 60 percent of the employees in these firms agreed that their work was adversely affected because their e-mails were not responded to in time or not at all. On the other hand, people complained that they receive too many e-mails each day to respond to them all.

Third, over 40 percent of the employees made their first impression of a person by the way they send their first e-mail, whether it be formal or informal, well or poorly written, short or long.

Fourth, the study revealed that companies need to formulate a clear internal policy, i.e., "netiquette" for using e-mail. Employees often complain that now and then they just cannot find the information they require from intranets. The reason for this is that intranets are often poorly designed and therefore not particularly user friendly. Consequently, this results in extra e-mail messages being generated about the topics in intranets.

Disadvantages of E-mail

If you receive fewer than 10 messages per day, it is not that important if some of these messages are so-called *trash mail*. These e-mails are often advertisements and are known as *spam* or unsolicited commercial e-mail. However, when you have to deal with dozens, possibly hundreds, of e-mails on a daily basis, the situation becomes totally different. If you receive 30 to 40 spam messages daily in addition to 50 to 250 work-related messages, you may become frustrated and annoyed. In addition, individual trash mails may be large and possibly contain highly contaminating viruses.

Another disadvantage of e-mails comes from the fact that not all people or companies have e-mail addresses and that one-third change their addresses annually. There are significant differences in e-mail availability among countries, especially developing countries. Simply having the wrong time on your PC might cause confusion among e-mail recipients, for example, your e-mail message might be placed at the bottom of their inbox. It is important to ensure that you have set the time on your computer correctly.

Employees often feel that e-mail communication is difficult. They are never sure if their e-mails should be short and to the point, or long and descriptive to eliminate the risk of misunderstanding or incorrect interpretation. Furthermore, some people do not like reading e-mails from the screen and consequently print them. As mentioned earlier, reading the original message from the monitor is almost one-third slower than reading the printed version—if digital reading techniques are not employed.

The internal network—intranet—may be misused for personal benefit. Employees may send e-mails offering personal items for sale, or they might send e-mails to all employees to cover themselves, avoiding the possible accusation of hiding "essential" information. In the old days, sending messages to everybody required a great deal of running around. If someone wanted to send a memo or message to a large group of people, he had to type up the memo, make copies, and distribute them physically. The steps involved in sending messages this way often ensured that they were only sent to people who really needed them. Hardly anyone was dedicated enough to photocopy hundreds of copies of a memo and circulate it to everyone in the organization. However, your e-mail inbox does not pose such physical challenges, and with a push of a button, any mail can be sent to as many people as you can fit in your address book. Consequently, e-mail overload is a growing problem that is rapidly reaching chronic proportions.

Advantages of E-mail

The reasons why e-mail has gained so much popularity as the primary communication tool are manyfold. Messages can be sent and read irrespective of time and place. Further processing of information sent or received is simple. Because messages are in a written format, you can arrange, file, transfer, classify, and manipulate (change font, add/delete text) individual messages in any way you want.

E-mail communication is considered a green, environmentally friendly media. It does not pollute (transportation, paper mills) and saves natural resources (trees). It allows instantaneous transmission of messages to anywhere in the world as the data moves with the speed of light. E-mail offers all these advantages at minimum cost.

The ever-increasing popularity of e-mail shows that its advantages clearly outweigh its disadvantages. It is therefore imperative that a solution be found to manage the growing number of e-mails in our inboxes.

ABCT² Analysis

Introduction to "Waste Management"

Take a look at Figure 4.2 below. Do you recognize the situation in your own life? Maybe in a colleague's life?

Figure 4.2: Principles of "waste management."

One of the hardest tasks for the above person is throwing something away. He applies this principle to all his incoming mail. He thinks that, if he throws something into the trashcan or deletes an e-mail, the very next day someone will want it. Therefore, he keeps everything, either in filing cabinets or drawers or on his computer. Most of it could be considered trash, but he lives by the saying: "Someday, someone will ask for that information—it's best to keep it."

He has adopted the management principle called "waste management." The underlying principle is to store "garbage" in places next to him. At home, what do we normally do with the garbage? Naturally, we throw it in trash containers. However, this man keeps this garbage at this worktable and spends his entire day in crisis mode. Because he is unable to prioritize, every task is both important and urgent.

Take a look at your worktable. Do you see any "garbage?"

In Figure 4.2, take a look at the time (8:20), which is a reflection of the position of the mouth. Notice there are two briefcases. What do you think is the purpose of the second briefcase? Maybe at the end of the day, he will take unread papers and other unfinished work home with him. Do you think he enjoys his working life? Possibly for him, burnout is waiting around the corner.

The picture of "waste management" may seem ridiculous and funny, at least at first glance. In the end, the principles depicted may prove to be very costly for the company. If the person in the picture is, for example, in charge of sales and thus dealing with customers, think about these questions:

- Would his decisions/offers have been better if he had had the time to read all the material related to the customer request or bid?

- Would the company have made more money if his decisions and offers had been based on all the available information about the competitive situation, market analysis, price levels, product qualities, economic indicators, etc.?

A-, B-, C-, and T^2-mail

One of the most efficient ways to manage the incoming flow of printed or electronic mail is to apply ABCT² analysis. This technique divides your mail and other tasks into four categories based on the criteria *important-urgent*. All mail is classified either important or not important, urgent or not urgent, from the *business point of view*. You need to consider if the task in question is important and urgent and whether its execution will lead to some kind of benefit for the company. This method will help you place your printed or electronic mail into four main categories: A, B, C, and T². The overall goal is to maximize the time spent on tasks in the top two quadrants and minimize the time spent on tasks in the bottom two quadrants. Figure 4.3 simplifies this division.

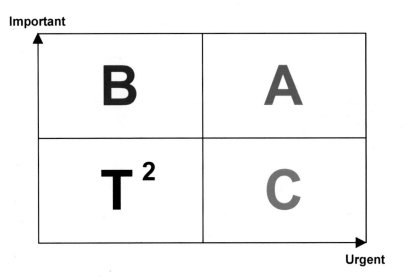

Important

Urgent

Figure 4.3: ABCT^2 analysis.

A-mail: Do it now! All mail that is important and urgent from your business point of view and requires almost immediate response is taken into the A-folder. This A-category consists of mail and tasks that require your action during that day, or at the latest within 24 hours. Items that could be classified in this category are, for example:

- A request, letter, or e-mail from your customer. Even though you may not be able to give the correct answer immediately, it pays off to send a quick message thanking the sender for their interest and informing them that you will get back later.

- A complaint from your customer. Here you need to react instantly. One customer left unsatisfied could mean losing up to 24 other customers. One happy customer will result in 8 more.

- A task from your boss (written or oral) to be carried out immediately. You can always ask yourself, What happens if I fail to do it on time?

- A bid due shortly. If you do not respond on time, your company can lose the deal and a great deal of money.

- Your input to a project. These tasks are especially important in teamwork where the progress of the whole project might depend on your producing a critical piece of information as early as possible.

- Production decisions, emergencies, other customer needs, various deadlines (could even be B-items turning into A-items).

These tasks are essential for the success of the business. You must react to these assignments during the next 24 hours or your business will suffer (see Figure 4.3).

B-mail: Allocate time to do it. All mail that is important but not urgent to your business can be transferred to the B-category. These are tasks that must be taken care of, but do not require an immediate action. You have flexibility to set aside some time to manage each B-task. To avoid crisis management, it is vital that you allocate sufficient time every day and every week to these important but not urgent B-items. Typical B-items include the examples listed below:

- developing a new product/service
- coaching
- completing a small part of a larger project
- implementing a major change process
- budgets, annual plans
- project and strategy planning
- personal/staff development
- writing reports, drawing out action plans
- visiting customers (not the urgent ones), etc.

All these are important and should be taken care of in order to run the business successfully on a long-term basis. However, anything in the top *left* quadrant that is not achieved will eventually make its way to the top *right* quadrant, and crisis management is ready to start (see Figure 4.3).

C-mail: Do it or delegate. All mail that is "urgent" but less important from the point of view of operating the business successfully is categorized as a C-item. These C-category items are fun-to-do, easy activities that act as "day fillers," but are definitely not productive. (This does not imply that the actual business is not enjoyable.) C-tasks include the following:

- all routine tasks
- daily administrative work
- making a phone call to a friend to plan the weekend
- tasks or favors to other people
- personal tasks
- e-mails full of jokes/animations from your friends
- reading the daily "gossip" newspapers

Typically, this category contains routine paperwork and the like, which requires relatively little input and very little effort to accomplish. Normally, you carry out C-tasks at any time, although you should handle these only after you have finished with A- and B-tasks. In addition, you have one more option: You may decide to *delegate* them; maybe somebody else in the organization can do the job.

T^2–mail: Dump it. T stands for trash. T^2 means that you should have two wastebaskets. The mail that is immediately designated as garbage is "crumpled" into the first wastebasket. The second wastebasket will be used for material that you dare not dispose of because you feel that one day you might need it. "Someday, somebody will ask for that information—it's best to keep it." However, *both* wastebaskets will be emptied in the evening. So next day, you can start from scratch with two empty wastebaskets.

What happens, however, if your nightmare comes true? You *did* throw away a paper that somebody needed the next day. Do not worry. More than likely, someone else in the organization who is still following the waste management principle will have a copy or the originator of the message will have one. If not, your $ABCT^2$ analysis may need to be sharpened; you need to review and look again at your key result areas.

The RISE Principle

After receiving incoming mail, quickly sort out the material. Handle each piece of mail separately. With printed mail, pick it up. With e-mail, open it up on the screen. Look at the item and classify it based on a quick general scanning. Because the amount of e-mail increases all the time, employ the four questions covered by the acronym RISE during your scanning process:

- **R**eceiver: Has the mail been sent to my address or am I part of a mailing group?

- **I**mportance: Does the subject line have any relevance to me? How does it relate to my present work? Is it part of my ongoing project?

- **S**ender: Who sent it? Do I know the sender?

- **E**xpected: All three above taken into consideration, is this e-mail something I have been waiting for?

Do not start reading the actual messages, but instead browse quickly through them, keeping RISE questions in mind all the time. Try to prioritize the information and decide where in the A-, B-, C-, or T^2-mail categories you will place it. At this point, handle each item only once. However, be careful not to transfer (scan) printed matter into electronic format just to make your desk look cleaner.

The Rule of 3Ds

If you receive between 50 and 150 or even more e-mails daily, you need to find a rational way to manage this obvious overload. Use the rule of *3Ds*—three easy-to-remember options with your mail:

1. Decrease—filter, automate, do not give out your address

2. Defer—prioritize with ABC, do not answer, let time take care of the issue

3. Delegate—pass on to others, routines, automatic answering

Even working on the conservative basis of allocating 30 to 60 seconds to deal with each message (this is a minimum, many messages will require far longer), you need to dedicate anywhere from one to three hours of work time simply to get through your inbox.

Pareto's principle. *Pareto's principle*—also known as the *80/20 rule*—states that 80 percent of your productivity comes from 20 percent of your tasks and vice versa. When 80 percent of the value comes from 20 percent of the capacity, the trick is to identify that key 20 percent. You should prioritize and put all your emphasis on this important 20 percent of tasks. A- and B-tasks belong in this 20 percent, and so do your key result areas. These are the main areas of your life, both at work and at home. You need to concentrate your time and other resources on these areas in order to achieve your goals. There is a temptation to allow C-category material to take priority over A- and B-material, because C-material is fun and fast to go through. Being "light," it also requires minimum thinking. The same applies to your T^2-category. Processing trash can actually be time consuming. Be aware of these two categories, because they can easily take up a big part of your day. Try to identify the productive 80 percent and allocate more time to manage tasks in this group. See Figure 4.4, which illustrates Pareto's principle.

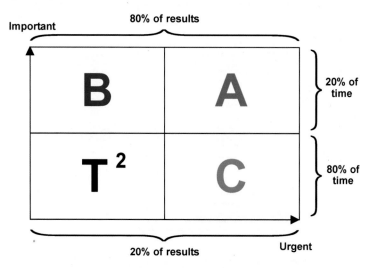

Figure 4.4: Pareto´s principle: The connection between mail and results.

Printed matter. You can immediately put ABCT^2 analysis into practice at your worktable. All you need are four filing trays of different colors stacked on top of each other. The top tray is colored red and all A-items are stored in it during the day. By the end of the day, it must be empty. The next tray is blue, and all your B-items are stored there. It does not have to be empty by the end of the day—not even by the end of the week. However, continuously monitor its contents and take care of B-tasks after you have completed A-tasks. As mentioned earlier, B-tasks tend to become A-tasks if not started in time.

The third tray is green, and all your C-items are stored there—tasks that are fun to do, but not important from a business point of view. You may start the C-tasks when the A-tray is empty and you have accomplished a sufficient number of B-tasks.

In the bottom tray, you will place all material already taken care of and waiting for archiving. By the end of the week, you should file these papers into the main filing system (archives, folders, cabinets, etc.). See Figure 4.5, which shows an example of an ABCT^2 filing system.

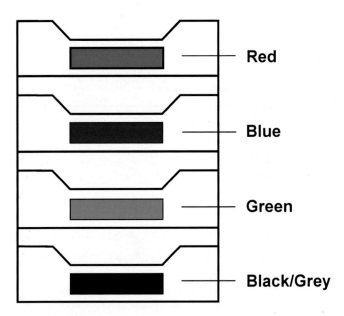

Red

Blue

Green

Black/Grey

Figure 4.5: Filing trays at your worktable will remind you to use ABCT² analysis.

E-mail. You can apply ABCT[2] analysis to e-mail by creating three subfolders under the inbox titled A, B, and C, as shown in Figure 4.6.

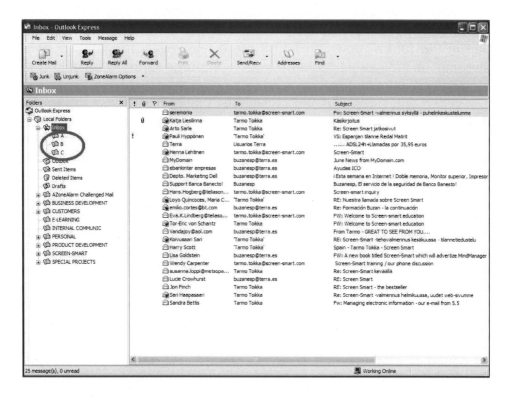

Figure 4.6: Applying ABCT[2] analysis to e-mail by creating three subfolders labeled A, B, and C.

When downloading e-mail from the server, do not start reading messages one by one. Instead, rapidly scan all of them by looking at the sender and subject line. Bear in mind the questions that were presented earlier: Who has sent the message? Do I expect it? Remember the acronym RISE: Receiver, Importance, Sender, and Expected.

All messages classified as A-mail—important and urgent, to be answered on the same day—are moved by dragging and dropping them into the A-subfolder. All messages regarded as B-mail—important, but not so urgent—can be moved into the B-subfolder. The rest—not important but "urgent"—goes into the C-subfolder or preferably, in many cases, you slide them directly into the *Deleted items* section—recycle bin. You can also activate the message and then push the delete button. The advantage of the recycle bin is that you don't have to empty it daily or weekly (especially if your computer has sufficient memory capacity). If you need the information in the future, you can find it there. However, monthly "housekeeping" is advisable to keep your computer running quickly and efficiently.

When you have finished classifying incoming e-mails, open the A-folder and start dealing with these messages immediately. After completing A-item e-mails, you can start with B-items, provided that you still have time left that you had allocated for checking e-mails. Only after acting on the e-mails in the A- and B-folders can you start scanning through your C-messages. Reserve time in your daily schedule to read and react to your incoming messages two to four times each day, anywhere from 10 minutes to 1 hour per session. However, be careful about becoming addicted to constantly checking your inbox; studies show that one-third of all e-mail users check their inbox more than 10 times a day.

Carrying out ABCT^2 analysis requires deep concentration and total elimination of distractions. One of these distractions is automatic notification of a new e-mail arriving. You may hear a particular sound or see a picture of an envelope flying across your screen. It is very hard not to look when you know that a new message has arrived. Turn off your automatic notification, because it will constantly interrupt your work. Most messages can wait a couple of hours, and you do not need to take measures immediately. It is not reasonable for a person sending an e-mail to expect you to reply immediately. If the subject matter is urgent, the sender will most likely get in touch with you either by phone or contacting you in person.

Folder Structure and Filing

Keeping up with e-mails is considered one of the worst causes of stress in the workplace today. Managers and other employees still do not know how to use e-mail systems properly. People are unable to cope with their workloads and often struggle to meet targets. A report by the British Department of Trade and Industry

(2005) found that workers spend an average of 49 minutes a day sorting out their inboxes. By comparison, working parents play with their children for only 25 minutes a day.

Leaders and trainers within organizations need to work with individual employees to identify and deal with the root causes of stress, and develop more efficient ways to manage e-mail overflow. One simple solution to start with is practicing housekeeping—"cleaning" your folders once a month at a minimum. Reserve a special time each month in your schedule to go through all your folders. Delete e-mails that are no longer important. Keep only the latest, up-to-date information stored in your files. Of course, you may clean your folders weekly, even daily. However, do not allow this to become a task that is done only once a year because it will then be insurmountable.

Another way to tackle the stress caused by e-mail overflow is to establish an efficient filing system right from the very beginning. Any system you select should support your natural way of remembering things. The short-term memory (mainly the conscious and the semiconscious memory) can remember a maximum of eight things (or eight bits) at one time. You should build your archiving system so that it does not exceed eight folders at one time (see Figure 4.7). Basic folders such as *Inbox, Outbox, Sent Items,* etc., are not included in these eight main folders. Design a folder structure with eight main folders and subsequent subfolders underneath these. Limit the number of subfolders to about half of the number of main folders. Each of the eight main folders has a maximum of four to five subfolders; each subfolder has again a maximum of two to four sub subfolders, etc. (see Figure 4.8). This system will make filing and searching for e-mails much easier because your folder structure now supports your brain's natural way of memorizing things.

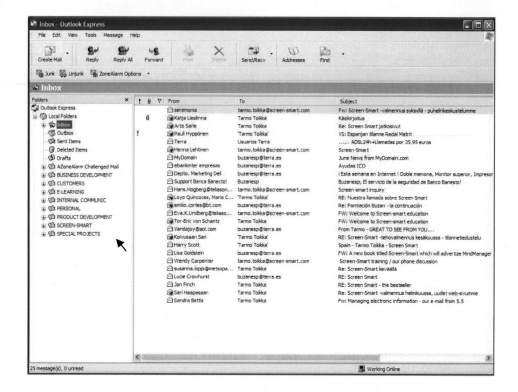

Figure 4.7: The 8-bit rule applied to the main folder structure supports memory.

Effective Screen Reading

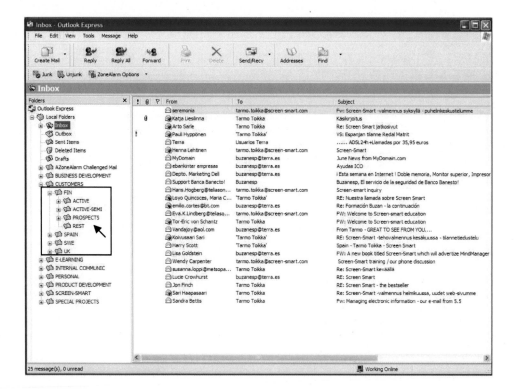

Figure 4.8: The 8-4-2 rule: limit the number of subfolders to a maximum of four.

By the end of the day, make sure your *Inbox* and *Sent Items* folders are empty and e-mails are stored in their respective folders (see Figures 4.9 and 4.10).

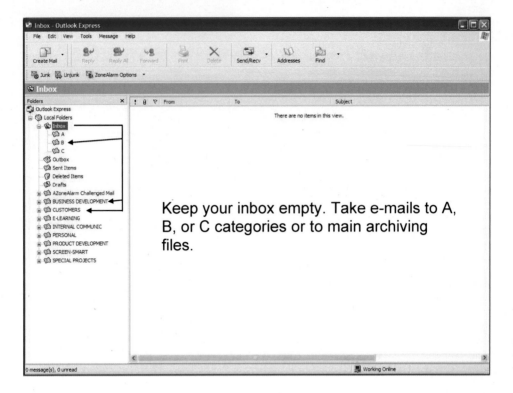

Figure 4.9: Good housekeeping requires the *Inbox* to be empty at the end of the day.

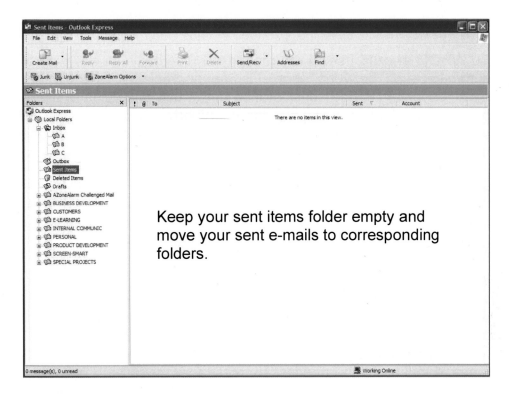

Figure 4.10: Good housekeeping requires *Sent Items* to be empty at the end of the day.

Developing E-mail Protocols

Due to the mass of e-mails, companies urgently need to introduce internal protocols and guidelines for using e-mail as the primary communication tool. These guidelines are, however, nothing revolutionary. Many strategies and processes used with other types of communication (phone, faxes, letters, etc.) apply the same way to e-mails. The potential overload of messages is related to the question of how employees want to communicate across teams and across whole organizations. The need is to develop guidelines and protocols on communication within the company and ensure that these rules are followed.

Consideration

To WHOM should I send the message? The basis for any type of communication between people is the appreciation of the other party, especially giving consideration to the use and value of his or her time. Not all e-mails are for everybody. Because e-mail is already an impersonal way of communicating, it becomes even less personal if sent to everybody in your address book. More and more people—especially senior executives—are complaining about this all-inclusiveness, i.e., receiving e-mails that do not concern them. Often people really do not understand what consequences may result from sending one message to various colleagues in the organization. Before pushing the *Reply All* button, count to 5.

WHAT should I send? Send only messages that need to be sent—messages containing information that adds value to the other party. Do not automatically assume that your e-mail is important and will be read by the receiver. People are often annoyed at receiving "important" e-mails with nothing to indicate this importance. Avoid sending unnecessary messages, such as "I agree…," "Your suggestion sounds good…," "You will soon receive an important e-mail…," unless the receiver specifically has requested an answer. Count to 10 before sending an unnecessary e-mail. By not sending it, you will often save your colleagues a lot of time. If possible, try to limit your e-mails to one topic/subject per message; this simplifies the communication. It is actually recommended to send more short e-mails than to incorporate many different topics into one message, which often makes the message long and complicated.

HOW should I send it? Bear in mind that besides e-mail, there are other ways to communicate. You can still use the traditional telephone—and/or cellular phone. You can also send a fax, and what an impression you will make on your client if he/she receives an "old fashioned" letter from you. At least you can rest assured that he will, in most cases, read it.

Sometimes face-to-face contact is necessary. This is especially true when negative feedback is being given. Constructive criticism of performance should never be delivered via an expressionless e-mail published in the company's intranet. Out of respect for the individual, matters like these should always be addressed face-to-face. Internal conflicts should never be settled using argumentative e-mails. If a serious disagreement about an issue erupts, it should be resolved over the telephone or by arranging a one-on-one meeting to avoid escalation.

An inappropriate tone in your e-mail can show lack of tact. Because e-mail messages tend to be short by their very nature, this shortness may be considered brusqueness, which may open the door to misinterpretation. In addition, remember that there are different manners and cultural variations. "Get-to-the-point" messages used commonly in Northern Europe and the United States may be thought of as impolite in Latin America and countries in Southern Europe. If you use e-mail in a multicultural environment, make sure you know the differences between cultures, and take time to write the message appropriately. This will guarantee that the receivers who originate from different cultures will read your mail and that they will understand it as you intended.

The Subject Line and Other Rules

Guidelines should be developed on how to write meaningful subject lines. On many occasions, this is one of the few areas *immediately* visible to the receiver. The value of your message at the receiver's end may totally depend on how you use the subject field. This can make a big difference and will determine if your mail is read or deleted instantly. When writing the subject line, make the title as descriptive and accurate as possible—better yet if your *complete message* can be entered in the subject field. Also, write the reason for sending the message in this field.

Always give a specific, clear answer to all questions. Refer to the sender's message, and attach relevant matters to each other. Leave a small reference before your text, but not the whole message. By writing your answer immediately after this, you connect the matters and make reading easy for the other party. Unfortunately, too often we receive messages where the answer is put on top and a copy of our message is situated below (and all previous messages below this). We have to read the answer and all the other messages just to check that the sender has not added anything in between or at the very bottom.

Be careful to whom you send copies of your e-mail correspondence. Only send copies to parties concerned or your e-mail correspondence can end up in the wrong hands.

Because e-mail reflects your presentation skills, always proof your message for spelling and grammar. If, for example, you are e-mailing an offer to a client and it contains grammatical mistakes and spelling errors, you will not make a good impression. Unfortunately, too many people write as they speak, which appears sloppy when read as a text. Use automatic spell checker for everything you send out to help avoid improper use of language.

People have a tendency to use too many words to express themselves. To avoid writing more than necessary, use short and clear paragraphs to separate different topics and facts from one another. This will give clarity to your presentation. If you decide to send a few pages of information, edit it beforehand. Use capital letters only to emphasize a matter or in headings. Using capital letters excessively will make the receiver think you are SHOUTING!!! Besides all capital letters are HARDER AND MORE TIME CONSUMING TO READ.

The general impression you give to the receiver will depend on the presentation of your e-mail without any doubt. Proper use of e-mail is not only the key to effective work practice, but it will project the right image and show respect for others.

Attachments

Many people have a tendency to send large documents as attachments without considering the inconvenience this might cause the receiver. There is also a potential virus risk involved in many types of attachments, and the receiver might have to scan your e-mail before opening it. Consequently, do not pass on chain and advertising letters, programs containing animations, or jokes, because these may contain macro viruses, Trojan horses, or other types of worms. Virus warnings received from unknown sources should be deleted and similarly not passed on, although the sender would like you to send the message to everybody in your address book. Often these warnings carry no relevant base, and their purpose is just to increase e-mail traffic on the Internet. In case of doubt, it is advisable to visit the pages of reputable antivirus companies to check on the current virus situation.

Another potential risk with attachments is that the receiver may not have the right application to open your message and it will appear on his screen in an illegible and confused format. Attachments are often large and require extra time to download. Try to incorporate the information in your MS Word and other documents as a part of your e-mail. In most cases, it is the actual contents that count and not the presentation format. If you really need to highlight and use special fonts, use *Rich Text Format (RTF)*. For internal company communication, large attachments (jpeg, tiff, ppt, doc, xls, mp3) should have their own server or other specific place in the intranet. In this way, attachments common to various people are stored only once and the link is given to the receivers.

Signature

Hardly any company allows employees to print their own letterhead or design their own company logo. It is important that everybody use the same form and logo when sending business letters to clients. However, when people at the same company send e-mails, one notices various types of endings (or signatures) including, for example, "smart" proverbs, quotations from movies, or lyrics from famous songs. If the sender then leaves out relevant information, like phone and address, trying to contact them later might prove to be very difficult.

All business messages sent from a company should bear the *same* signature format. This includes greeting, official company name, name of the person sending the message, his/her title, company address, phone (direct and mobile), fax, e-mail, and Web address in this order. All correspondence must contain these elements, and no additional information like proverbs or quotations are allowed. Many e-mail programs allow you to add the signature automatically. However, be careful when using a ready-made letterhead in RTF. Your customer's software might not be able to open it.

Smileys

E-mail is most often a straightforward, short, and "get-to-the-point" type of communication. Because e-mail lacks emotional expressions, people have developed symbols—smileys—to express their moods. Most commonly used are :-) for happiness and :-(for being sad. You should be careful when using these in your business correspondence, because they might lead to incorrect interpretation, differences in opinions, and other types of conflicts. The receiving party could even consider that you are not taking the matter seriously. Avoid abbreviations such as "FYI" (for your information), "IMHO" (in my humble opinion), "FWIW" (for what it's worth), "IMNSHO" (in my not so humble opinion). Preferably, do not use them at all.

Text Format, Long Messages

The main purpose for e-mail communication in business is to send and receive information. The most reliable way to carry this out is to use *Plain Text Format*, which is supported by 100 percent of all e-mail programs (see Figure 4.11). Plain text will guarantee that your message is always readable at the receiving end. Additional benefit will result from the fact that sending and receiving times will be shorter, which will save money. Rich text format may not always be supported by the receiver's equipment, and your message may be jumbled at the receiving end.

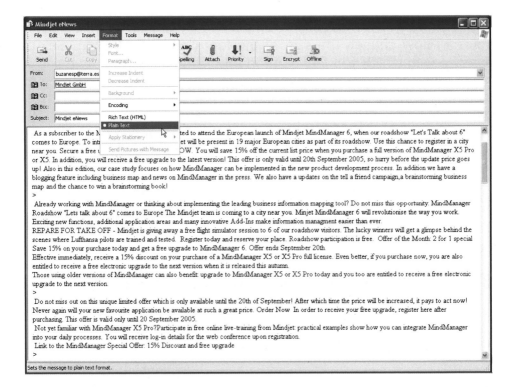

Figure 4.11: Select *Plain Text* as a basis for your e-mail messages.

How to read long e-mails quickly. Now and then people claim they have not received an e-mail (which they actually *did* receive). This is one of the most common e-mail "sins" today and generally rises out of a sense of guilt for not having replied. The reasons for not answering can be many, but the fact remains that a great deal of business is lost because of it. One reason for being "economical with the truth" is the lack of time available to read long e-mails.

Ideally, e-mails should contain a maximum of 20 to 25 lines or about 200 words. You can apply the ABCT[2] analysis explained earlier to these types of short messages, because they do not require any type of "manipulation" (i.e., changing the text style). When you start going through the A-folder, you should apply all the techniques of digital reading. However, the situation is different if you receive e-mails that have a lot of content. Besides the basic speed reading techniques presented in Chapter 2, here are some additional tools to assist you with long e-mails.

Right click the mouse and *Select All*. By activating all the text, you can now change the size of the font (*View, Text Size*). Select the size with which you feel comfortable. Remember that by using a small font, your eyes are able to grasp more information with each fixation. However, print that is too small can be difficult to read. Test your vision capacity.

Another method you could try is to click on the *Reply to Sender*. You will now have the availability of *Rich Text Format*. By right clicking your mouse and *Select All,* you may now change the black color of the text to your preferred color. You also have the option to change the font size and the font type to increase the readability. Try to find the optimum combination for these parameters (see Figures 4.12 through 4.16).

Figure 4.12: Click reply to have access to *Rich Text Format* in order to "manipulate" the text

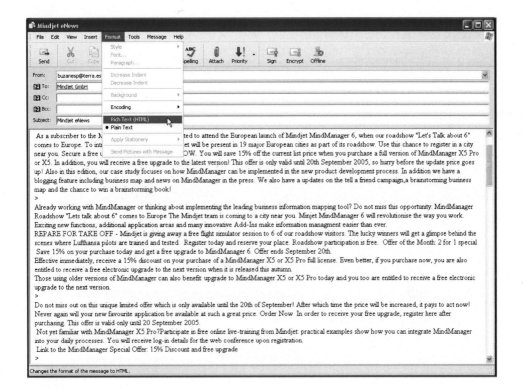

Figure 4.13: Click on *Rich Text* to have access to font size and colors.

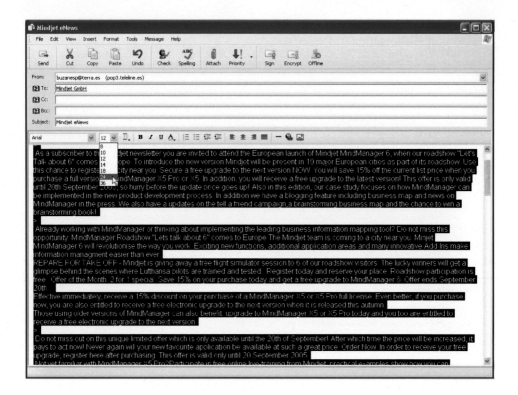

Figure 4.14: Select *All* from *Edit* or right click the mouse. Increase the font size to reduce the number of words per line, which makes text more readable.

Effective Screen Reading

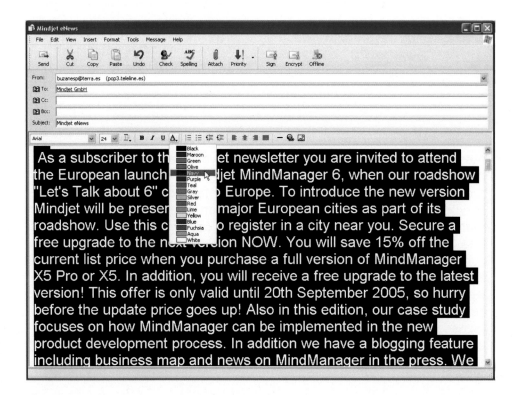

Figure 4.15: Select your favorite reading color. Start reading with only a few fixations per line, often even one stop is enough. Use any type of guide such as a laser pointer or the cursor of the mouse, which shows the center line

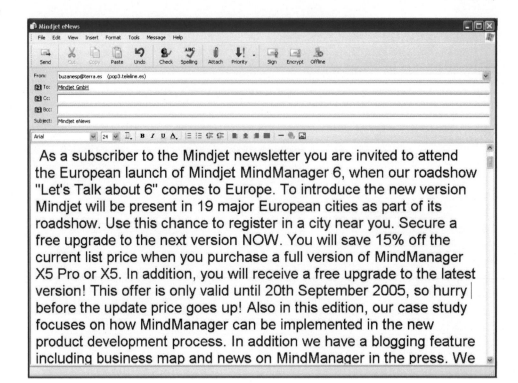

Figure 4.16: The end result—the manipulated text.

Summary and Onward

E-mail addresses and the amount of electronic mail are growing rapidly. Reading daily messages requires more and more time and more and more e-mails need to be answered. Efficient time- and self-management techniques are required to overcome this problem. ABCT[2] analysis offers a simple solution for the management of both printed and electronic data. Its principles are applicable to all types of e-mail configurations. Time savings and reductions in stress levels with this analysis are evident. The next chapter will deal with the other digital time consumer—the Internet.

— 5 —

Manage the Internet

This chapter will offer a three-step fundamental approach to help you log on to the Internet (the Web) and use it. The Internet offers a definite competitive advantage to those who know how to manage and use the system correctly. You need to know how the Web works and its advantages for fast information retrieval. Your ability to set goals and action plans can be crucial when reading online or off. A dozen practical tools to assist in your Internet sessions will be presented. We will show four different ways to read Web pages—skimming, scanning, exploring, and in-depth—and which one to select for different page layouts. At the end of the chapter, the latest developments in search engines will be presented, and tips for more efficient searches are given.

The surge and spread of the Internet has been compared to the inventions of both electricity and the automobile. This information network of millions of computers has already had such an impact on our daily lives, even though we are just at the beginning of this era of cyber space informatics.

It is estimated that there are between 850 to 950 million Internet users currently in the world. Roughly 60 million host computers in more than 250 countries are connected to the Internet, and its traffic is *doubling* every three months. Although there are more than 800 million personal computers in use today, the real market is estimated to be over four times bigger. By the end of 2007, over 1 billion people will be connected to the Internet.

More and more traditional commerce is done over the Web. For the year 2006, B2B (business to business) e-commerce alone was topping $300 billion. Consequently, you have to learn how to use the Internet in the most efficient way.

Manage the System

One should understand what the Internet is and how it works in order to use it efficiently. There are various books and Web pages explaining this topic, but since our primary objective is not about the mechanics of the Internet, we will touch on this subject only briefly.

How the Internet Works

The Internet is a huge, worldwide network of computers connected to one another through existing telephone lines. The transfer of information between these computers is extremely efficient. Plans are underway to construct a new fiber optic cable across the Atlantic Ocean with a transfer capacity of 2,400 gigabytes per second. This technology will allow the transfer of 1 million television pictures simultaneously on the Net.

Typically, access to this network takes place via a computer with a modem. In many cases, you need a contract with a local company that serves as your Internet Service Provider (ISP). The ISP will act as your host, and you can connect your computer to the Internet through its lines and server. The part of the Internet that organizes and distributes the vast amount of information available on the Web is called the www—the World Wide Web. All documents on the www are referred to as pages. Each page has its own Web address referred to as URL (Uniform Resource Locator). This is the code used to identify Web pages and other information on the Net.

Hardware. The development of the actual system configuration is changing all the time. Commercial versions are available with the equipment to access the Internet just by using an ordinary TV—without the need for a computer. Various companies (Microsoft, Sony) offer set-top boxes for interactive cable television or for just accessing the Internet through the television monitor. A set-top box, which acts as add-on terminal to the TV, is plugged in, and by operating a remote control unit, immediate access to the services offered by the Internet is obtained. The extra terminal normally contains a modem, www-browser, electronic mails for data and voice, card station for a smart card (which contains user data, password, connection details, etc.), and a remote control unit.

Yet another type of configuration is on the market from mobile phone manufacturers (e.g., Motorola, Siemens, Nokia, among others). Flat screen cellular phones with a built-in keyboard and the capability to access the Internet with just the push of a button are becoming more and more common.

Faxes. The Internet also offers the alternative to send faxes. This is especially important for organizations that are reluctant to accept electronic information and require proof on paper. Some telecommunication operators offer services specifically aimed at transferring faxes on the Internet. In addition to the benefits of increased speed and savings in telephone costs and paper, this configuration opens up the opportunity for mass mailings. Furthermore, incoming phone lines are not occupied when faxes are sent or received.

Fast information retrieval. The main advantage of the Internet is to offer extremely fast information retrieval. The Web is a massive library of information, offering instant access to almost any type of data. You access the most up-to-date information available because the majority of documents appearing on the Web are dated.

Extremely powerful search engines will find the information basically on any topic. The capacity of these "super searchers" for storing and retrieving information in a fraction of a second from the vast pool of interconnected computers worldwide is unprecedented. Of all the computer power ever built in the world, 90 percent has come online in only the past few years. Some scientists go to the extreme and predict that by 2021, a $1,000 computer will match the processing power of the human brain.

Side effects. Some words of warning on the negative sides of the Internet should be mentioned. In 1995, the phrase *Internet addiction* was first coined, and by the start of this millennium, alarming reports indicated that excessive Internet use could also cause serious depression, combined with deep feelings of loneliness and separation. Internet addiction refers to people who actually cannot "live" without a daily or nightly session on the Internet. Their social life becomes minimal, normal duties at home are forgotten, and they are totally exhausted during the daytime while at school or at work. This is a new, serious illness, which can take many months to cure.

Set Vision, Goals, and Action Plan

If you decide to spend your leisure time on the Internet, then it really does not matter what you find and how long you spend surfing. It is no different than indulging yourself on a beautiful Sunday morning with a cup of coffee and a donut while reading your favorite newspaper. You can easily spend an hour on the front page, and after putting the paper down, still not remember the headlines. The same thing can also happen with the Web. People simply select a page at random and start reading. Often this starting point is referred to as "a portal," which offers connections to various topics. After one topic, they click to another connection and move on to that. These people use no strategies whatsoever to extract and remember information and vital points.

However, if using the Web is part of your work and "time is money," you should have the three-step fundamental approach illustrated in Figure 5.1 in mind before going on and for the whole time you are on the Internet.

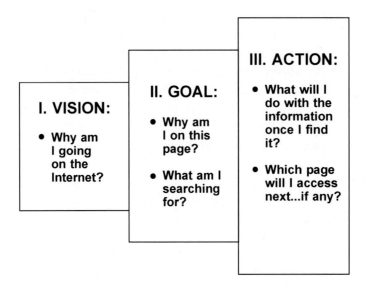

Figure 5.1: Three-step approach for your Internet session.

Vision. Before opening the connection or even the browser, you should ask yourself the following question: *Why am I going on the Internet?*

Having some kind of vision—an overall view in mind before you start—will considerably help you achieve your goals during Web sessions.

Goal. Stating a goal in advance will lay the fundamental foundation for your Internet session. A clearly defined goal or objective will set your mind to the topic in question and help you retrieve information from pages much faster than without a clear mind setting. By visualizing the whole picture, it will be easier to find those pieces of information that are relevant.

As the Web is flooded with information, it is of the utmost importance to determine whether a document opening up on the computer screen will be helpful and useful in achieving your initial goal. Keep the purpose clearly in your mind all the time and you are able to quickly scan for key words, source of authority, date of publication, and other pertinent information that will determine the value of the page *at that moment.*

Action plan. Using the Internet is not free. The equipment (PC, modem, etc.) to access the network costs money. The services of the Internet Service Provider costs money; they charge either a monthly, fixed fee with unlimited use of the network or a fee based on the usage. The use of phone lines, cable, or DSL costs money.

While it is true that the market is forcing ISPs to offer very competitive connection charges—some even provide free connection—the biggest cost undoubtedly is *your time.* All the time you spend on reading information—be it from the Internet or from other sources—is "wasted" unless it results in some *concrete action.* This action must have a tangible benefit to you or to your organization either immediately or in the near future, such as writing a report to your manager, making a short summary for a board meeting, completing a research study, or sending an interesting article to a potential customer. These are all tangible results to the questions: Why am I reading this? What will I do with the information?

Options for Reading

When you find a Web page that contains relevant information, you have three options:

1. To read the text online and take notes

2. To download the page to your computer, save it, and then read it off line

3. To print the information as a backup, and read it in the traditional manner

A majority of Internet reading is "rereading" or "scanning" (see "Scanning" in this chapter). Know what you are looking for and go directly to links or subtopics that are truly useful from your point of view. Some articles you may want to read online; others you may prefer to download and file them to read at a more convenient time. The decision mainly depends on *how much time you have available* at that moment.

You can set up some means of monitoring your online time with on-screen reminders offered by some Internet Service Providers. If this is not available, perhaps the alarm function of a watch or a clock will do. Scan what you wish to read off line as quickly as possible and store the information while, at the same time, delete insignificant documents. Keep track of time, and focus on using sources and content effectively.

Be aware that some pages cannot be downloaded with the *Save As* command so that it can be read off line later. If all you want is to store the information, i.e., the text on the page, the following procedure is recommended:

- Only activate the text.
- Click the right mouse button and then click *Copy.*
- Create a new document.
- Paste the text to this document.
- Give it a destination and a name.
- Save the document in a selected folder with the *Save As* command.

Many pages have a "printer friendly version" option. This will make saving the document much faster, and reading the document directly from the screen will be easier.

What next? Once you have made up your mind what to do with the information on the Web page, you need to decide where to go next. No single standard, rule of thumb, right or wrong path exists when moving from one page to another (backward or forward) within a multiple-page Internet document. It all depends on why you originally logged on to the Web.

By clicking commands, such as *Go to, Next Page* or *Previous Page,* it is possible to move around inside a document. You might need additional information and have to open up new links. Maybe you have found what you have been looking for and it is time to exit. Alternatively, you might want to return to a previous location within a document or sub address. Identify the appropriate icon that will take you there, place the arrow on the desired site, and click.

A Dozen Tools for the Internet Session

Keep the goal for your Internet session crystal clear in your mind at all times, because it will always determine the next step. If not, you end up clicking from one "interesting" connection to another and find yourself totally distracted from the original mission. Besides the vision, goal, and action plan, there are other elements and tools that will make your reading and finding information on the Web faster. We will present a dozen techniques and ideas to assist you in making your Internet sessions more productive.

Fixations

In Chapter 2, we explained how the eyes move. In order to read, the eyes must stop on words in the text. These stops are called *fixations.* The same rule applies to text on a screen as it does to printed text. Try to limit your fixations to a maximum of two to three stops per line. Many times the text is placed in such narrow columns that even one stop per line is enough. Shorten the fixation time and keep moving forward.

An example of how to use digital reading techniques with a typical Web page is given in Figure 5.2. Limit your fixations to only one per line, and focus your attention in the middle of the line.

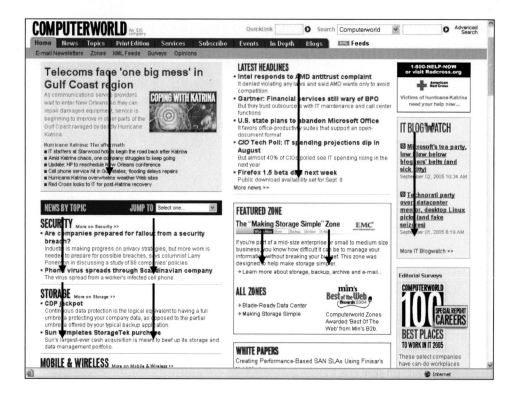

Figure 5.2: Fixations. Read a Web page with one or at the most two fixations per line. The arrows indicate the recommended eye movement.

Initial Scroll

What happens with your eyes when you open up a new Web page? Most often, the first few seconds are wasted, because your eyes try to fixate on different elements on the page. They make a sporadic movement, criss-crossing the text lines and other elements on the screen, before starting to read the actual words.

The more advertisements, banners, pop-up windows, and moving animations the page layout contains, the more difficult it is to find the key information quickly. On average, we spend one or two seconds on each new page just *beginning* to read it.

Knowing how the eyes move on the screen is naturally of great value to Web page designers who decide the location of banners and other elements. The more distracting elements that are placed in the upper part and corners of a Web page, the more inclined the reader is to notice and click on these. (See Figure 5.3, which illustrates eye movement on a Web page.)

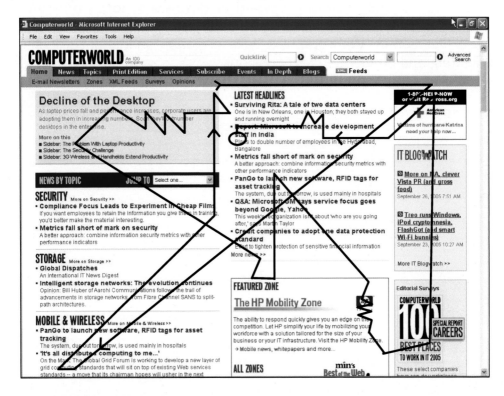

Figure 5.3: Initial eye movement on a Web page (dark line). No information comes in during this phase.

Consequently, the reader will be distracted away from the original purpose for opening up the page. Be aware of these distractions and make a conscious effort to concentrate knowingly in the middle of the page.

To get the big picture and achieve maximum comprehension efficiency on a Web page, it is always advisable to carry out *a rapid scroll,* i.e., to scroll down the whole page quickly. If the whole page is not visible at the same screen shot, an overview obtained by using rapid scroll will help you understand the general theme of the contents. Initial scroll can be accomplished by hitting the space bar one stroke at a time.

You can also use the scrolling device in your mouse. Some mouse types will even allow you to adjust the number of lines for each touch. When scrolling upward or downward, focus on either the top or the center of your screen for maximum comprehension (see Figure 5.4). With graphics, take a global "snapshot" of icons, pictures, and condensed text positions.

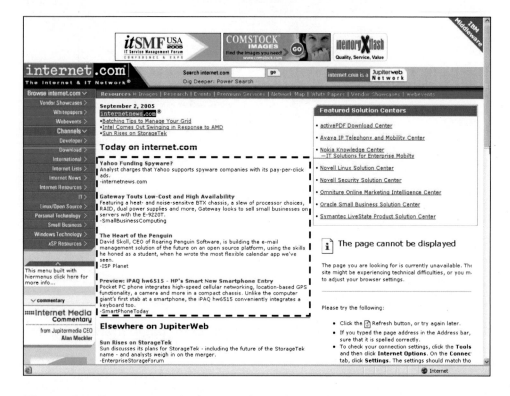

Figure 5.4: Recommended area of concentration.

You should quickly go through the home page and the links to obtain a general idea of *all* the pages involved. As mentioned previously, to have the big picture in mind will make it easier to attach any new information to the old existing database.

Page Elements and Browser Shortcuts

You must understand the structure of a Web page and know the elements, their meaning, and how they interact with one another. Memorize the toolbar and icon positions for rapid printing. Use the

Effective Screen Reading

Help function if a command fails. Type toolbar commands accurately. Memorize the location of frequently used icons and commands. Reflex action can prove to be your most effective tool on the Internet.

Know the most typical browser and other (Windows) shortcuts to minimize the use of the mouse and to improve ergonomics in your work (see Figure 5.5, which lists shortcuts). There are many times when you can accomplish the same function much faster with a shortcut than trying to position the cursor of the mouse on the icon and then clicking.

Browser Shortcuts	
Alt + left arrow	Back
Alt + right arrow	Forward
Ctrl + B	Favorites or Bookmarks window
Ctrl + D	New favorite
Ctrl + F	Find dialog box
Ctrl + H	History
Ctrl + N	New browser window
Ctrl + O	URL window
Esc	Stop
Space bar	Scroll down one screen length
Ctrl + E	Search in Explorer bar
Alt + D	Text in Address bar
F4	Recently visited sites
The Windows Key	
Windows	Start menu
Windows + R	Run dialog box
Windows + F1	Help
Windows + E	Windows Exploring
Windows + F	Find/Search Files or Folders
Windows + D	Minimize all/undo minimize all

Figure 5.5: Typical browser and other shortcuts.

Junk Information

Not everything on the Internet is true and worth reading. Learn to recognize pages of real value from those with less importance.

Always check details on the organization, company, or individual who has produced the Web page. If you have any doubts about the contents, move on to other pages.

The same applies to e-mails: your mailbox can easily get filled with junk mail. Use ABCT[2] analysis and scan each title in a single sweep. If neither the title nor the sender seems familiar, move on by pressing the delete button (see Figure 5.6) or put the mail into the recycle bin (see Chapter 4, "Waste Management"). To delete multiple messages, hold down the *Shift* key (for consecutive messages) or *Control* key (for random messages) on those items to be deleted. This will activate all messages selected and they can be deleted with only one click.

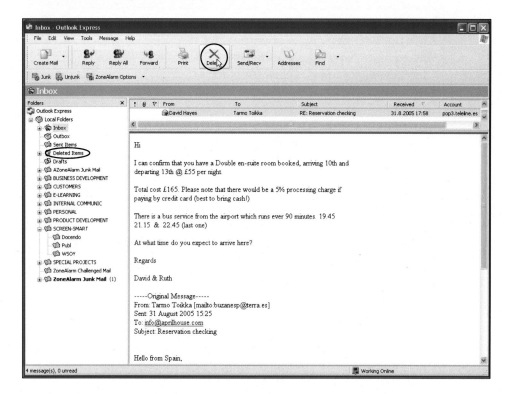

Figure 5.6: Deleting options with e-mail (Outlook Express).

When on the Internet, you do not have to be afraid that you will accidentally delete or lose valuable information. You are asked twice whether or not you really want to exit a site, make a change,

Effective Screen Reading

or get rid of the information. Most programs have built-in verification prompts of OK for a second and final chance to make the selection. The next screen will always take you where the last screen left off.

Password List

Some Internet pages and services, either free or payable, require user identification (i.e., giving your name and password) before allowing access to the information on those pages. Generally, passwords and codes are required for the following:

- code number for credit card
- customer number for net bank
- PIN-code for mobile phone
- code for mobile answering service
- code for passage control at work
- on and off codes for burglar alarms at work and at home
- user password to enter PC
- user password for local area network
- password for screen saver
- user passwords for different computer programs
- code of child locking device at home for the TV and video
- password for the Internet and other Net services

As the number of codes and passwords is constantly growing, people select an easy-to-remember password, and use the same one for all different services. However, the disclosure of this code will expose all equipment and Web services to potential danger from third parties all at the same time. Try to avoid, therefore, the multiple use of just one password, and consider the following points when deciding on new ones.

A good password is

- at least 8 characters long;
- a mixture of characters, not only letters of the alphabet;
- not a word in any language, not even conjugated;
- not a name, nickname, or name of a pet;
- not an ID-number, a car registration plate, or other code;
- not derived from other passwords.

If you have difficulties remembering several passwords, keep a list in your wallet or in some other secure place for quick access. The list can be a piece of paper or an electronic document in your computer. Make sure that you write down whenever you add a new password to your list.

There are programs available that use just one password to give you access to your other passwords. However, be aware that your company may have strict rules on writing down passwords. Check these first and follow them.

Favorites

One of the fastest means to re-enter a useful Web page is to bookmark it and add it to your *Favorites (Bookmarks)*. When you have found an interesting page that you want to return to later, click on *Favorites,* give the page a name, and add it to your *Favorites* (see Figure 5.7).

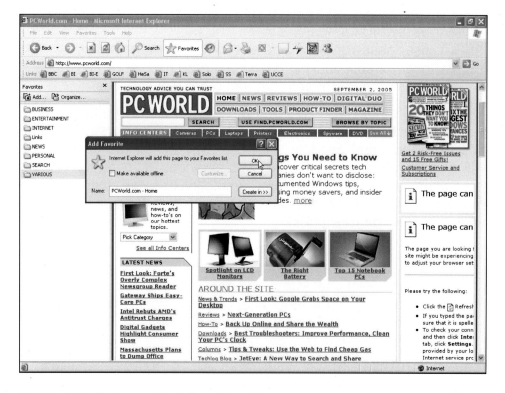

Figure 5.7: Using and adding favorites.

Keep the main categories and their subsequent subcategories in Favorites to a maximum of eight. Remember that your conscious and semi-conscious memory can deal with a maximum of eight bits of information. If you arrange your favorites to support your memory in this manner, you will find the required addresses faster since memorizing the overall structure is easier. Organize all new favorites under these eight main categories and add new subcategories—when necessary—keeping their number preferably to four or under (see Chapter 4). Keep a clear and concise structure. See Figures 5.8 and 5.9, which illustrate categories organized under *Favorites*.

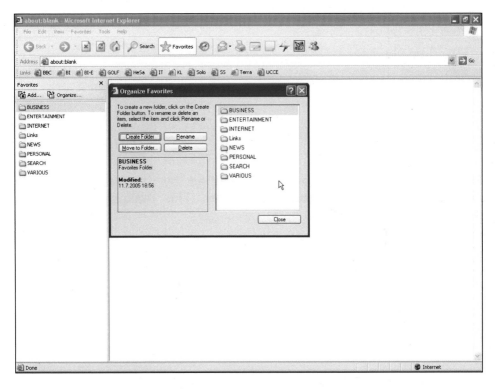

Figure 5.8: The use of a maximum of eight main categories in *Favorites* will support your natural memory.

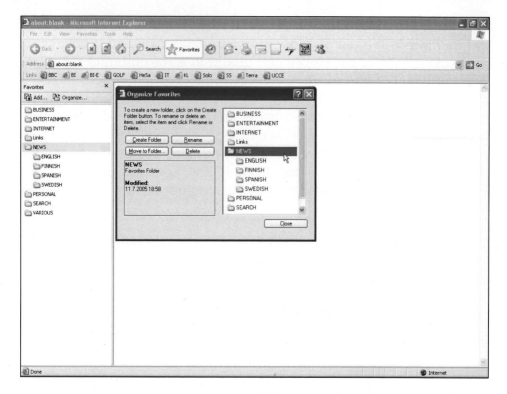

Figure 5.9: *News* category is classified by language. You can concentrate on one language at a time. This makes your reading faster and comprehension better.

Effective Screen Reading

Manipulating the Text

The manipulation of a text means that you change the original text font and the background to be more attractive and appealing to make reading faster and more efficient. If you are not happy with the text layout on a Web page, change it. By giving it a more user friendly look, reading the text will be quicker and easier, and you will remember more. This is especially important if the text is long.

After copying a text from a Web page to a Word document, change the font to one that is more attractive to your eyes. Select your favorite size and type by testing with a larger and darker letter size. This change results in fewer words per line and, consequently, will reduce the number of fixations per line.

You can also highlight the whole text in your favorite color. This will make the text attractive to the eye, and define it with restricted borders. The eyes will catch the form and borders of text lines faster, which will again increase your reading efficiency. Besides highlighting the text, you can also change the text itself to your favorite color, or you may want to color just the key points by double-clicking a word.

Various combinations are available for the text and background color: black text on yellow background, dark blue text on light blue background, or brown text on light green background.

To summarize:

- Change the font size and type. Test with larger and **darker** letters. This will reduce the amount of fixations per line. Use your favorite style of letter like **arial black**, **verdana,** or `courier`.

- Highlight the whole text with your favorite color. This will define the text with restricted borders. This will help the eye catch the form of the line faster for increased reading speed.

- Color the text itself with your favorite color.

- Do both at the same time.

- Color just key words by double clicking the word.

- Try various combinations with the background; find your favorite one and use it.

You might also try different spacing of lines from the *Format, Paragraph* controls. However, it should be noted that when reading, single line spacing is the most efficient, because the eye can grasp chunks of information at one fixation (see Figure 5.10).

Line Spacing		
Single	**Space-and-a-half**	**Double**
The manipulation of the text will help you read faster and understand the contents better. When you read the text on a Web page and want to make a summary, you can combine text manipulation and a mind mapping program. Below is an example of text manipulation to identify the required key elements from the text:	The manipulation of the text will help you read faster and understand the contents better. When you read the text on a Web page and want to make a summary, you can combine text manipulation and a mind mapping program. Below is an example of text manipulation to identify the required key elements from the text:	The manipulation of the text will help you read faster and understand the contents better. When you read the text on a Web page and want to make a summary, you can combine text manipulation and a mind mapping program. Below is an example of text manipulation to identify the required key elements from the text:

Figure 5.10: Using single, one and a half, or double line spacing. The eyes read faster using single line spacing.

Effective Screen Reading

Step 1: *Select an article*. From a selected Web page, copy an interesting article.

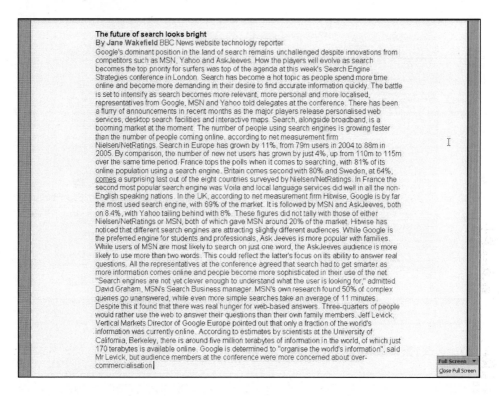

Picture 5.11. Select an article.

Step 2: *Manipulate the text*. Activate all (*Select All*), make it larger (*Font 16*), change the style (*Arial Black*), use color (blue) and highlighting (yellow). These changes will make the text more attractive and faster to read because you need fewer fixations per line. You can read rhythmically and your comprehension will increase as the right side of your brain is activated.

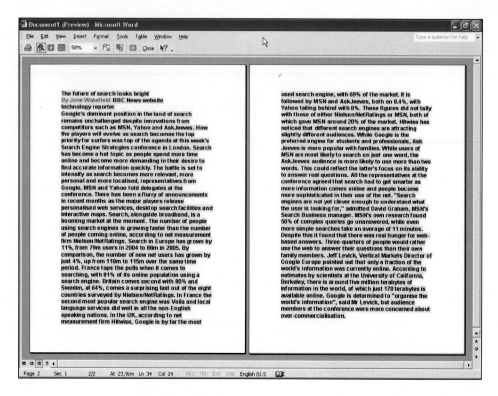

Figure 5.12: Manipulate the text.

Step 3: *Find key words*. Search for the most important elements in the text. Use one color (red) for individual key words and highlight key ideas with another color (green). Develop your own color coding and take advantage of different symbols, arrows, lines, etc.

Effective Screen Reading

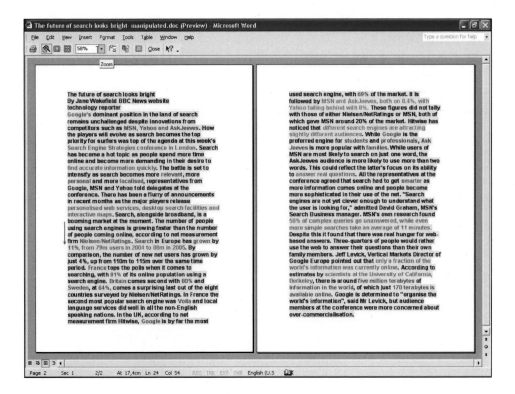

Figure 5.13: Find key words.

Step 4: *Make a summary*. Open MindManager (or another) program to assist in summarizing the article. Divide the screen into two halves (MindManager, Word) and start importing (by clicking and dragging) the key words and elements from the text directly into your map in MindManager to summarize the article. You do not have to write anything; just add symbols and pictures from the symbol gallery.

When you close the Word document, do not click on the command *Save Changes to the Document* if you want to keep the original text.

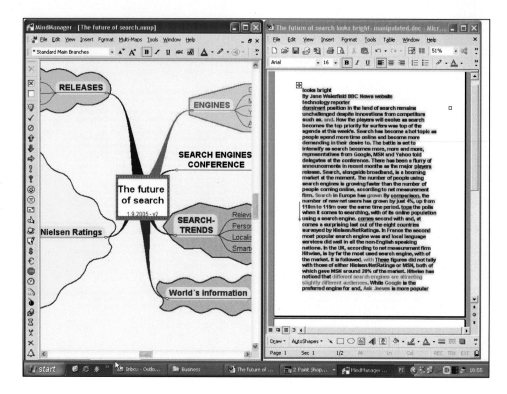

Figure 5.14: Make a summary.

Step 5: *The end result*. During the whole process, nothing has been printed. You have been working online all the time, taking advantage of various "tricks" that your computer software offers. If you wish, you can now print the summary made from the article. This is the end result in a mind map form.

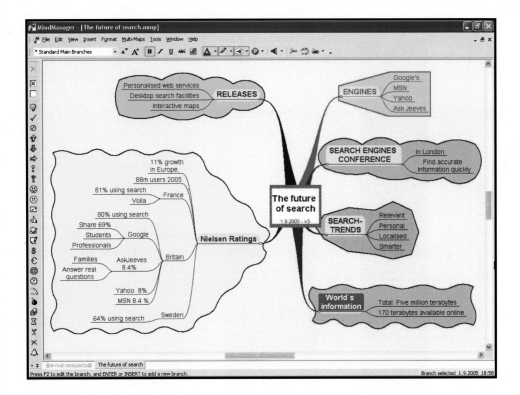

Figure 5.15: The end result.

Advantage of color coding. Various tests have shown that the use of colors can improve your memory anywhere from 10 to 30 percent, and possibly even more.

Eye movement cameras clearly demonstrate that using bigger letters and color will contribute to faster information retrieval from a computer screen. Increase in the letter size by 40 percent drops the search time to half. Furthermore, if the key word is colored, the search time is only one-tenth of the original. Color coding is especially useful when you quickly screen search result lists. See Figure 5.16, which illustrates these data.

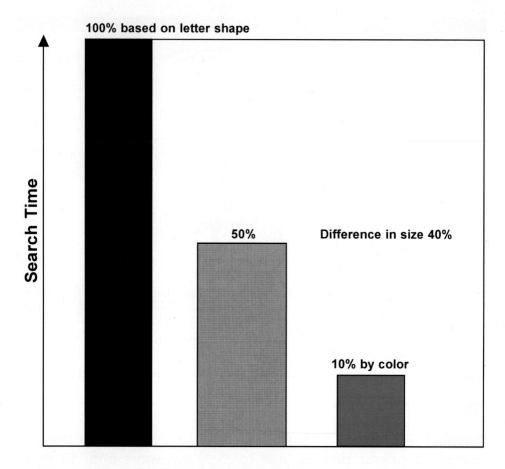

Figure 5.16: The difference in search time when using 40 percent bigger font size or color on a computer screen.

You can also manipulate the text (see Figures 5.17 and 5.18) on a Web page by using special programs (for example Front Page from Microsoft).

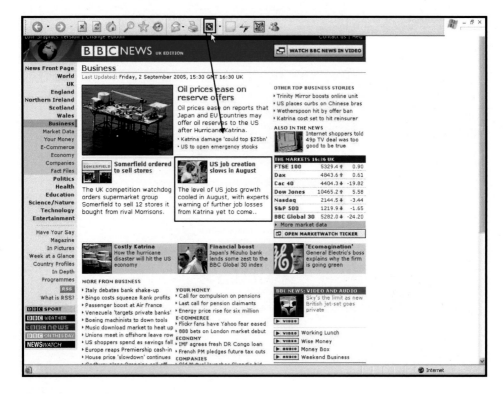

Figure 5.17: The original Web page.

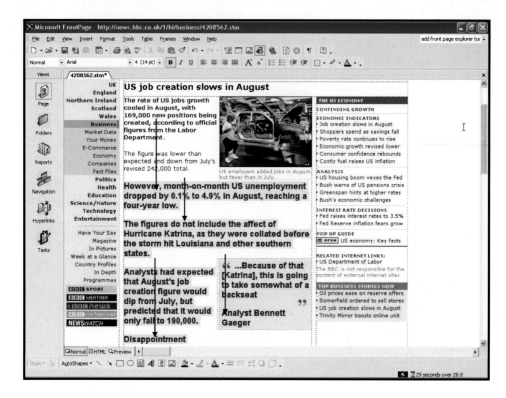

Figure 5.18: An example of Front Page software. You can directly manipulate the text on the screen for increased legibility. Only one fixation per line of text is necessary.

Key Words

Finding key information from Web pages is a major challenge. However, by maintaining a clear objective, you are much less likely to read word by word. What the eyes capture, the mind can process, providing you stay focused on your goal. When the mind knows precisely what you want and need, it will automatically start working toward the realization of this goal. Consequently, your chances to locate necessary key words will be greatly enhanced. Once you identify key words, remember to accentuate (silently) them to aid connections and memory.

Effectively managing on-screen layout requires a full use of one's abilities. Information is retrieved from a page both in a visual and psychological way. To benefit most from the Internet, you should know, as specifically as possible, the key words, that can take you directly to the correct source of information while searching through this massive global library.

Know where to point the arrow, mouse, or glider. Use the browser to find a particular word or phrase quickly in a long text. Simply click the command *Find* and type in what you are looking for (see Figures 5.19 and 5.20).

Writing styles for the Web are much more likely to be abbreviated, concise, and more to the point than traditional print because of space constraints. Use peripheral vision and rely on the use of synonyms. Keep a thesaurus close by when conducting a search and reviewing your findings.

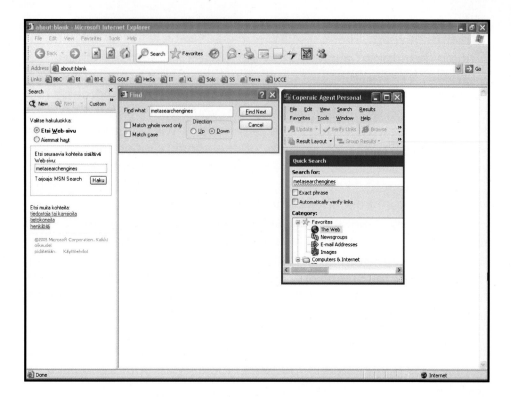

Figure 5.19: Using the *Search* or *Find* functions on Internet Explorer to retrieve the required information faster.

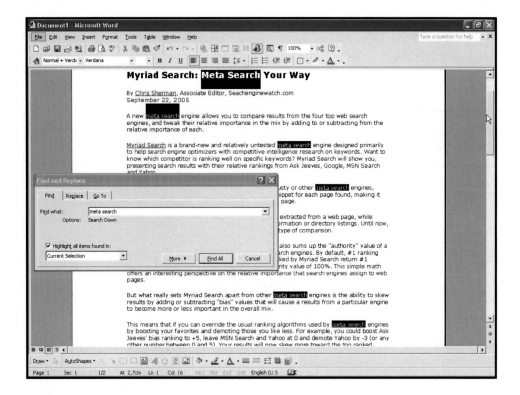

Figure 5.20: By using the *Find* function, time is saved because it is not necessary to read the whole document.

CS Guide

Use a pointer, laser pen, or cursor as a pacing tool when reading text on a computer screen (see Figure 5.21). Your eyes work more efficiently with assistance. In Chapter 2, we explained how to benefit from a CS guide or the mouse arrow. When using the cursor as a pointer, focus on the right side of each line as you move down the screen. If you use a laser pointer, the beam can serve as an effective underlining device to track each line of print. The vertical scroll bar on the right side allows you to move a single line of print or a full screen at a time.

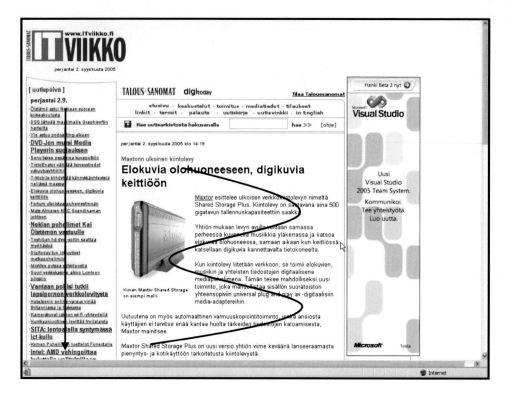

Figure 5.21: Use of scroll bars, the mouse arrow, and a CS guide or laser pointer. The movement of eyes is faster and reading is quicker.

Regression is less likely for a Web reader who uses some type of guide. It forces your eyes to move as quickly as they can through the text so that you take in larger "bytes" of type. Practice this until your hand-eye coordination is smooth. In addition, your capability of locating precisely what you need at any given moment will increase.

Remove Distracting Page Elements

Any movement on the screen will catch the eyes first because of peripheral vision. Pop-up windows, animations, flashing pictures, and other effects are guaranteed to attract your attention immediately. Therefore, it is advisable to get rid of these page elements as they most often

- are related to advertisements;
- appear first on the screen;

- take a lot of time to download;
- contain insignificant information.

There are special programs available on the market to "wash" and "clean" Web pages of ads. WebWasher from Siemens is one to mention. However, you need to download these programs, adjust and alter the software to suit your specific requirements, and even pay a licensing fee.

One easy way to get rid of ads is to go directly to your browser settings and remove certain default values. In Internet Explorer, you need to go to the *Internet Options, Advanced* tab and turn off *Play Animations, Play Sounds, Play Videos, Show Pictures*. This will remove all distracting advertising and other irrelevant material. Only the "clean" text will stay on the page. You will notice a definite improvement in your browsing, because you will download and read pages faster. See Figures 5.22 through 5.24, which illustrate this process.

(Source: www.mtv3.fi)

Figure 5.22: The original Web page with no change in default values.

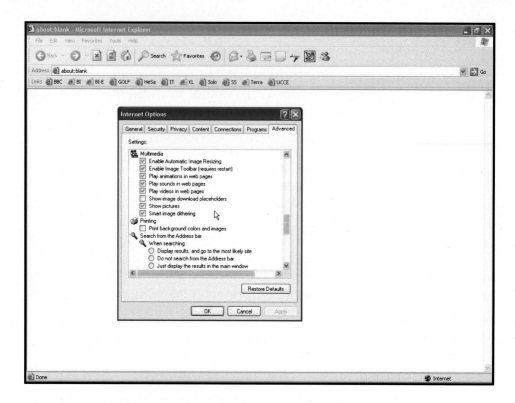

Figure 5.23: Turn off default values.

Effective Screen Reading

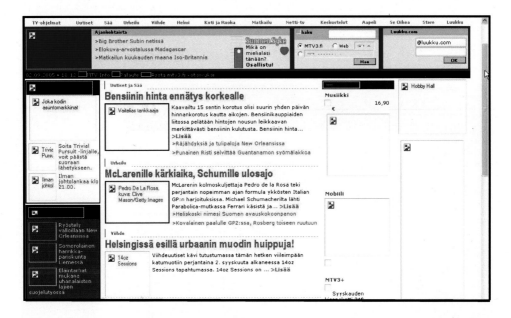

Figure 5.24: The "washed" image.

Use Supporting Programs

Keep your eyes and ears open to study the latest developments in the Internet. Actively read books and magazines describing new technologies, products, and other areas of interest. Keep your equipment up-to-date and benefit from programs designed to assist in surfing and information searching on the Internet (MindManager, MicroSurfer, AceReader, Copernic, etc). Learn how to use the Web most effectively, and you will be way ahead of the rest. See Figures 5.25 through 5.27 for examples.

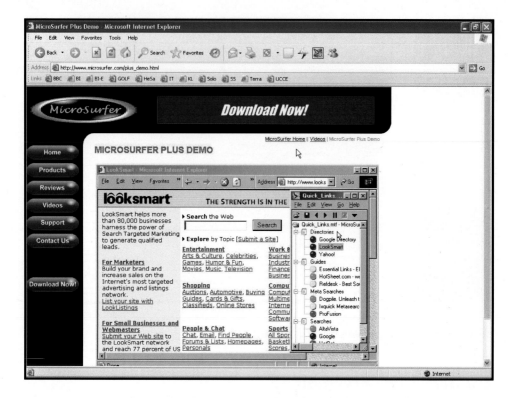

Figure 5.25: Use MicroSurfer (www.microsurfer.com) program to speed up reading. If the URL is not available, the program will notify you and you will save time by skipping this page.

Effective Screen Reading

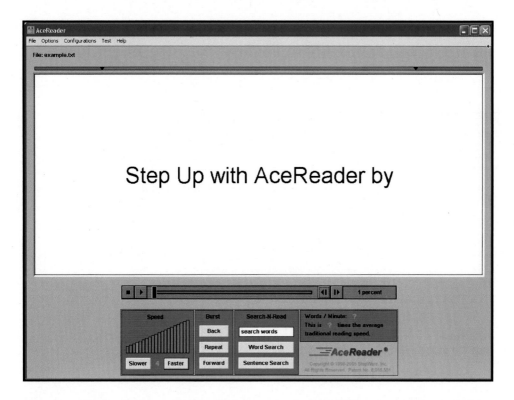

Figure 5.26: The main page of AceReader program (www. acereader.com). AceReader can be used to practice digital reading and to read long texts or Web pages quickly.

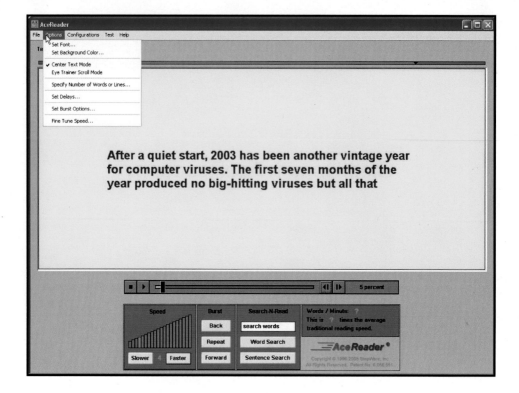

Figure 5.27: The options in AceReader software are versatile.

AceReader offers flexibility in reading from the screen. You can change the reading speed from 100 up to 2,000 words per minute. The options section offers versatility in adjusting the font color, style, and size. In addition, you can select your favorite background color and the length of the text line depending on the size of your focused vision. After some practice, you can even read multiple lines at the same time. By hiding bottom controls, the whole screen area is available for the text.

Page Layouts

Since various people and companies from all over the world publish pages on the Web, there is a massive number of different page layouts available with variable quality and trustworthiness. These pages vary from fast-to-load black and white texts to extremely elaborate, artistic displays with moving symbols, pop-up windows, and pictures, which sometimes seem to take forever to open.

Effective Screen Reading

Typically, there is a row of icons running on the left side and/or on the top of the page. Often the meaning of these icons is written on the bottom of the page or is displayed when they are pointed at. The text runs either in one, two, or three columns in the middle of the page.

Learn to recognize different page layouts and find the necessary connections quickly. Sometimes it can take a long time for the main page to appear on your screen due to large pictures and animations. Place the mouse arrow on top of any icon, and you will see text appear describing the contents of that icon. Do not wait for the main page to show up completely if you believe that the icon contains the information you are looking for. Click on it and move forward since you can always return to the main page. For the text, remember to use all the digital speed reading techniques explained earlier in this book.

Selecting the Right Approach

Always define your purpose or goal when you start reading a new Web page: Why am I reading this? What am I searching for? Depending on your purpose, select the right approach—either skimming, scanning, exploring, or in-depth reading—or a combination of two or more. Your selection will depend on the following:

- your reading goal
- the situation
  - your mood
  - time of day
  - distractions
  - lighting conditions
- the reading material
  - printed vs. electronic
  - type and placement of the text
  - page Layout
  - difficulty of the material
  - the number of pages
- the time available
  - short of time
  - plenty of time

People often find their worktable awash with different types of reading material and are literally surrounded by an ocean of information. This often consists of small details such as phone messages, notes made during phone discussions, customer contact information, ideas under development, work to be finished, plans, lists of material to be acquired, and of course, visible and invisible stacks of papers waiting to be read. These stacks consist of both domestic and foreign newspapers; trade journals on information technology, telecommunications, marketing, etc.; business reports on sales, costs, personnel, etc.; text and business books in both printed and electronic formats; e-mail received and sent; information on the Web on the development and general trends in your industry; digital newspapers; and so on.

Figure 5.28 will help you manage all the above information in an orderly and businesslike fashion. First, you need to decide the urgency and importance of the material with ABCT^2 analysis explained in Chapter 4. With practice, you will learn which approach is the most appropriate for the type of material in question. The main approaches that you can select are *skimming, scanning, exploring,* or *in-depth reading* or a combination of two or more. Some material might end up directly in your wastebasket or filing cabinet. Your aim is not to read all the material in the same way, but to be in a position where you are qualified to change your approach and reading speed to suit different material.

Material Available	Reading Approaches						
	ABCT^2	Skimming	Scanning	Exploring	In-Depth	Trash	File
Newspapers • Domestic • Foreign							
Trade Journals • IT • Telecomm. • Business							
Reports • Sales • Costs							
Books • Text • Business							
E-mail							
Internet • Competition • Digital news • Surfing							
Intranet							
Advertising							

Figure 5.28: Different reading approaches—skimming, scanning, exploring, in-depth reading—in relation to the types of reading material available.

Skimming

For the majority of Web pages, skimming is the most beneficial technique to apply. Let your eyes catch the headlines and captions. Pay attention to first paragraphs of articles and view potential summary sections. (See Figure 5.29, which shows eye movement when skimming a Web page.) Skimming Web pages is different from skimming printed matter because pictures appearing on the screen are normally advertisements. In books, you should always pay attention to pictures because they often contain key information in an easily understandable form. In the digital world, you skip pictures. Skimming will reveal which articles should be saved for further reading off line and which ones really are not for you. By adopting this approach, you will efficiently manage all types of Web pages, and quickly gain an overview on relevant ones.

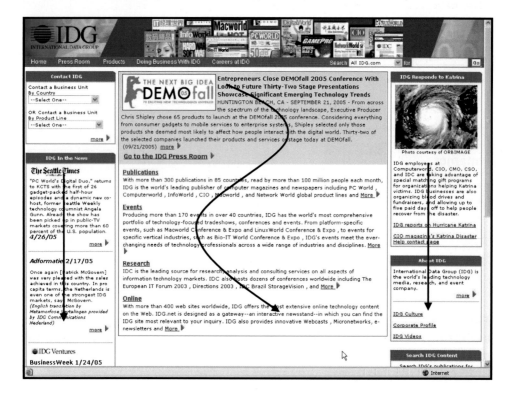

Figure 5.29: Skimming a Web page. The lines indicate eye movement. Fixations are mainly in the headings.

Scanning

Imagine that you receive an e-mail that has a 50-page report attached. It would be so easy to file it with the rest of your long, un-read e-mails. To cope with the situation, do a quick scan. First, tune your mind to the topic of the report by using the applied imagination technique (see Chapter 2.). Second, look for specific keywords, special names/areas, and specific terms. Third, as the brain is tuned to assist the eyes to spot those items, practice and develop your eye-brain coordination. Have your mind tuned in, and your eyes will identify the required information as though it was in bold print. You consciously need to sharpen and hone your awareness. Make an effort to scan pages at a glance and trust that your brain *will* recognize salient facts. Highlight with color those areas of a report that are interesting and appropriate for your work. Delete those parts that you do not need.

Save time by using the *Find* command. Type in the key word and it will be automatically highlighted in the text you are going through. You can then concentrate on this part and discard the rest (see Figures 5.30 and 5.31).

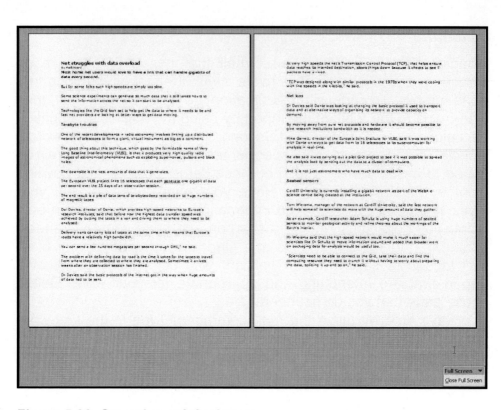

Figure 5.30: Scanning original texts.

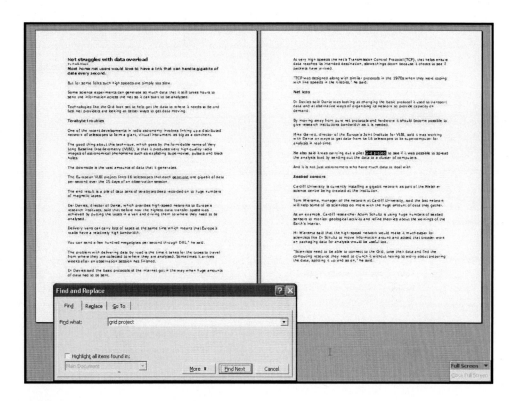

Figure 5.31: Scanning. With the *Find* command you can immediately locate where the key term is mentioned and concentrate on this section.

Exploring DigiBrowse

The term *exploring* generally refers to a technique used to gain control over a large Web site. When you open a new home page, you often encounter a multitude of different links inside the site and to pages associated with this site. To gain control over the information, you need to do a *DigiBrowse* (see Chapter 1, "SuperBrowse"). This means that you quickly open up all the links on that particular Web site one after another. The goal is to select in advance those topics or pages that are relevant from *your* point of view and only bookmark these. DigiBrowse will help you remain up-to-date with the "hot links" for your company and with developments in your particular area of interest (see Figure 5.32).

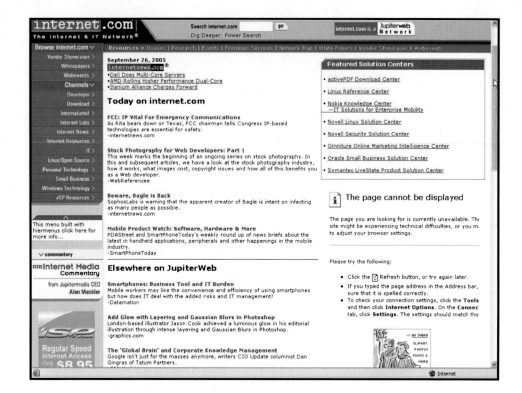

Figure 5.32: DigiBrowse. You decide which pages to reject and which ones to select for further exploration.

With DigiBrowse, you decide which pages to reject and which ones to select.

You can *reject* pages and information that

- you already know;
- offer similar case studies;
- appear illogical, weak, or inconsistent;
- offer irrelevant applications;
- offer neither details about the publisher nor the credibility of the author.

You should *select* pages that offer

- new information;
- new methods and applications for problem solving and decision making;
- links requiring further reflecting.

Do not discount and underestimate pages with unusual or surprising angles or viewpoints. These can sometimes generate brilliant ideas.

In-depth Reading

If you have found a Web page that seems to be useful, you may decide to read it through from the beginning to the end. The text may appear to be well written, the source may be reliable, or the information presented may be up-to-date and valuable to you from a business point of view. Perhaps the page is interesting for personal reasons. No matter what your reason is for deciding to read the text in-depth, always remember to use the digital reading techniques explained in Chapter 2.

Figure 5.33 shows that different information sources require different reading approaches. Not all material should be read in the same way, and variable approaches can and should be used based on the depth of details required and time available.

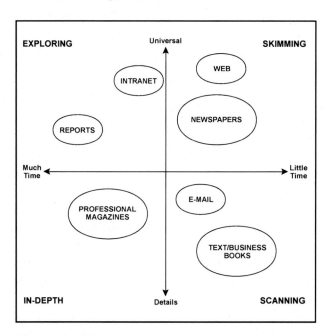

Figure 5.33: A simplified X-Y axis on how information sources and reading approaches vary in relation to time available and required depth of details. Each individual will personalize his/her own X-Y axis.

Search Engines on the Internet

In 2000, the estimations on the number of registered Web pages varied from around 4 to 5 billion. However, when the actual calculation was done in 2002, scientists discovered that many more pages existed than had been previously believed: the search found over 550 billion pages. The amount of new pages is obviously accelerating all the time.

There is so much information on the Web that any single search tool can only find a fraction of it. More than 20,000 different search engines are currently available. These search tools often specialize in particular areas and their use differs from one another, as does their coverage across the Web. For example, AltaVista can index about 2 to 3 billion addresses, while Google has a coverage of about 7 to 8 billion pages. However, even the best search engine will only cover a fraction of the total.

It is no wonder, therefore, that a special "breed" of search tools—*metasearchengines*—has emerged. These engines use various individual utilities at the same time. In a metasearch, Web search engines are simultaneously put to work together. When confronting today's mass of information, we are almost compelled to resort to these "wonder machines."

Search Tips—Stop Searching and Start Finding

Closely follow what new developments take place, and use only the most effective tools. Check regularly the recent news from Search Engine Watch (www.searchenginewatch.com), which also carries a listing on specialty search engines. Use the right tool for your search and you will find what you want quickly and effectively. If you have difficulties finding key words, but know in which category the item belongs, you can resort to engines (such as Yahoo) that show pages hierarchically in vast themes. If you want to have plenty of results, HotBot and AltaVista are effective in showing a multitude of pages. However, if your search is of a special nature, you should find a "specialist" engine. These are small, limited search tools that often have expert knowledge in narrow subject areas.

Observe accuracy and write exact key words and phrases in the search field. Avoid using general words, because these will give you a vast amount of results. When you encounter problems like receiving too many hits or wrong pages, sharpen your search and add different key words. If you search by phrase, remember to use quotation marks. These normally correspond to the exact order of words and therefore often produce the desired results. Remember that your spelling of names must be correct. If available, use specific languages for your search, and learn to use Boolean operators (AND, OR, NOT) correctly.

When too many hits appear, modify your search with new key words. Although the difference may be slight, make a new start and try other search utilities, like metasearchengines. They will produce many results in a relatively small amount of time. Some of the most popular include MetaCrawler, Ixquick, Profusion, SurfWax, and Copernic. The first four on the list are ordinary Web pages, the last one (Copernic) is a program and must be downloaded to your computer. Both SurfWax and Copernic include additional software that will make short summaries of the pages selected. This enables the reader to concentrate on key information, thus saving time. Besides, there is no need to read through the whole text.

Summary and Onward

In this chapter, you have learned various techniques on how to use the Internet more efficiently. We described how the Internet works and why it is important to set vision, goals, and/or an action plan when surfing the Net. We offered a dozen tools for your Internet sessions, for example correctly using fixations on lines, benefiting from initial scrolling, and understanding page elements. To support your natural memory, we showed how to use favorites and how the manipulation of the text will help your comprehension. Finding key words fast in the text and applying your CS guide were also demonstrated. Understanding different page layouts serves as the key for reading Web pages effectively. We demonstrated how to select the right approach for your reading with skimming, scanning, exploring, and in-depth reading techniques. Finally, the latest Web search techniques and tips were presented.

— 6 —
Summary

In the final chapter of *Effective Screen Reading,* we will summarize the entire book. This is imperative since reviewing is of utmost value in helping your brain remember all the new material and techniques presented.

Effective Screen Reading Objectives

Our aim has been to offer you concrete techniques to speed read e-mails and other documents from your computer screen, without the need to print the actual text. This is achieved through digital reading ability, which will also increase your understanding of the text and improve memory. Our primary goal is to improve your speed to capture the knowledge you require so that you can find key information more rapidly from the overwhelming mass of electronic data available on the Internet. With our easy-to-use, concrete techniques, you can select, scan, understand, and remember key messages far easier from now on. *Effective Screen Reading* strives to improve your personal productivity, allowing you to manage your e-mails and the Internet much more effectively. You will also learn how to significantly reduce work-related stress, because you will put more emphasis on ergonomic factors and strive for a better and safer working environment.

Effective Screen Reading

Almost everybody uses computers today. It is an essential element in a modern working environment. Consequently, effective screen reading is imperative for today's employees no matter what industry they work in. The solid foundation for effective screen reading is achieved with the DIRECT program, which encapsulates the main effective screen reading techniques:

- 3S technique based on using the TripleSpeed method
- CS technique for using a computer screen guide
- Pyramidal technique for taking advantage of peripheral and focused vision for maximum vision capacity
- Right brain technique, relying on rhythm, imagination, and mind setting
- PDS technique for placing yourself correctly in front of the computer screen—to optimize your position, distance, and mental strength
- Turbo technique based on the relativistic nature of the brain in maintaining high speeds naturally

Screen Reading Environment

Take a look at your work environment. A poorly designed and equipped workplace can reduce your digital reading efficiency more than 50 percent. Your ability to concentrate and understand what you are reading will depend greatly on your motivation, your knowing your body's optimum performance periods, your ability to maintain positive attitude, and your having enough well-planned breaks during the workday.

Ergonomic factors should always be taken into consideration when dealing with the computer screen reading environment. Positioning of lighting fixtures as well as contrast, resolution, and flickering of the computer monitor must be taken into account. Proper equipment, including the table, chair, display unit, keyboard, and the mouse, is essential. Increasingly, interest is being focused on the actual work environment with regard to air quality, temperature, atmosphere, sounds, and distractions.

E-mail

The vast majority of businesspeople consider e-mail to be the number one communication tool today. The advantages of e-mail are evident. However, there is an urgent need for effective management of e-mail both on the individual and corporate levels. Proper use of e-mail systems will be the key to productive work practice.

Not only is the management of e-mail flow essential, but also writing e-mails correctly is paramount.

If you receive 50 to 150 or even more e-mails per day, you need to find a rational way to manage this obvious overload. To start with, you can use the rule of 3Ds: three easy-to-remember alternatives to use with your mail system—decrease, defer or delegate.

The acronym *RISE* (easily remembered since the amount of e-mail is rising all the time) involves four questions, which you have to ask yourself while going through your inbox (the scanning process):

- **R**eceiver: Am I the principal receiver of the e-mail or am I part of a mailing group?

- **I**mportance: Is this e-mail part of my ongoing project?

- **S**ender: Who has sent it? Do I know the sender?

- **E**xpected: Is this e-mail something I have been waiting for?

You have learned how to use ABCT^2 analysis for both printed matter and e-mail for better time and self-management. This technique will help you prioritize your incoming mail and find key messages much faster, while freeing you from "waste management." ABCT^2 analysis divides your incoming e-mail into four different categories—A, B, C, and T^2—based on the importance and urgency of the mail in question. With A-mail, you do it now. With B-mail, you allocate time to do it later. With C-mail, you either do it now or delegate it. With T^2-mail, you dump it!

Bear in mind Pareto´s principle, which is also known as the 80/20 rule. It states that 80 percent of your productivity comes from 20 percent of your e-mail and vice versa. The trick is to find that 20 percent and devote more time to these e-mails. ABCT^2 analysis offers an excellent tool for this.

Construct your e-mail archiving system in such a way that it will support your *natural* memory. Besides basic folders such as *Inbox, Outbox, Sent Items, Drafts,* and *Deleted Items*, you should not have more than eight main folders. Try to limit the number of subfolders under these main folders to a maximum of four and thereafter to two, following the principle of 8–4–2. This will help you keep a concise structure, and you will find messages faster, therefore, saving time.

Due to the overflow of e-mails, companies need to introduce internal protocols and guidelines for using e-mail. A corporate e-mail policy should be formulated, with special attention being paid to precision, politeness, efficiency, security, and trust. This "e-mail netiquette" should cover topics such as subject line, length and contents, style of language, cultural differences, folder structure and their management, use of attachments, uniform signature, smileys, text format especially with long messages, recognition of suspicious messages, and confidentiality of e-mail messages.

The Internet

The latest estimation of worldwide use of the Internet stands at close to 950 million surfers—15 percent of the world's population is connected to the Internet. Experts claim that the Internet traffic is now doubling every three months. The total number of PCs in use is estimated at more than 800 million units worldwide and will easily top 1 billion in 2008. The number of Web pages is approaching the 1 trillion mark.

When surfing and finding information from this vast database, you should have a three-step approach in mind both before going on and for the whole time you are on the Internet. These steps are vision, goal, and action plan. First, set a vision and ask yourself: Why am I going on the Internet? Second, define a clear goal that will set your mind to the topic and help you retrieve information from the pages quickly. Third, make sure that your reading results in some concrete action that has a tangible benefit for you or for your organization.

Three options are available for reading Web pages: the text can be read online by taking notes, it can be downloaded and read off line, or it can be printed as a backup and read later on.

You can use various tools during your Internet sessions. Try to limit your fixations to a maximum of two to three stops per line, but preferably reading the lines by stopping only one time. The knowledge on how the eyes move across the screen is of great value, because we normally spend an additional 1 to 2 seconds on each new page when we are just beginning to read it. To appreciate the big picture and achieve maximum comprehension efficiency, it is always advisable to carry out a quick, initial scroll of the Web page.

Condition yourself to understand the page structure, and know the elements on the page, their meaning, and how they interact with one another. Recognize pages of real value, skipping those with spurious information and those of less importance.

Internet services often require user identification with passwords and codes. To increase security, avoid the multiple use of just one password.

When using favorites, keep the main categories and their subcategories to a maximum of eight. This type of hierarchical structure will support the memory, as conscious and semi-conscious memory can deal with a maximum of eight bits of information. In this manner, you will find the required addresses much faster, since memorizing the overall structure becomes easier.

When reading long texts, you should "manipulate" the text to give it a more readable appearance. By manipulation, we mean altering the style of the text to make it more legible and, at the same time, more user friendly. You can change the font, its color, and even highlight it. All this will make the reading faster and more efficient.

When you have the purpose for reading clear in your mind, you are much less likely to read word by word. Remember key words, because on the Internet, writing styles are much more likely to be abbreviated, concise, and more to the point than in traditional print, simply because of space constraints. Additionally, use a CS guide, laser pen, or cursor as a pacing tool when reading text on a computer screen. Your eyes will work more efficiently if they are being helped.

Remove distracting page elements, such as pop-up windows, animations, flashing pictures, and other effects, that are designed to attract your attention first and that most of the time contain insignificant information. Keep your equipment up-to-date and benefit from programs designed to assist in surfing and information searching on the Internet. Be aware that there is a massive number and variety of page layouts available. Learn to recognize different page layouts and find the required connections quickly.

Digital reading approaches include skimming, scanning, exploring, and in-depth reading. To select the right one depends on your reading goal, the reading material, and the time available. For the majority of Web pages, skimming is the most powerful technique to apply. With scanning, you need to consciously sharpen and hone your awareness and change your habits to allow yourself to scan pages at a glance. With exploring, you gain control over a large Web site. Home pages often have a multitude of different links inside the site and to pages associated with the site. To gain control over the information, you need to explore the page with a technique called DigiBrowse.

Single search tools can only find a fraction of the information on the Web. You should stop searching and finally start finding. Closely follow what new developments take place with search engines, and use only the most effective tools such as meta-searchengines, which use various individual utilities at the same time.

References

Books

Bates, W. (1995). *Better eyesight without glasses.* Thorsons.

Buzan, T. (1996). *Use your memory.* BBC Worldwide Publishing.

Buzan, T. (1995). *Use your head.* BBC Worldwide Publishing.

Buzan, T. (1991). *Speed reading.* First Plume Printing.

Buzan, T., & Buzan, B. (1995). *The mind map book.* BBC Worldwide Publishing.

Coman, M. J., & Heavers, K. L. (1998). *Improving reading comprehension and speed, skimming and scanning, reading for pleasure.* NTC Publishing Group.

Escarpanter, J. (1995). *Lea muy rápidamente.* Editorial Playor.

Frank, S. (1992). *The Evelyn Wood 7-day speed reading & learning program.* First Avon Books Printing.

Frank, S. (1998). *Speed reading secrets.* Adams Media Corporation.

Hall, D., & Wecker, D. (1995). *Jump start your brain.* Warner Books.

Hermann, N. (1996). *The whole brain business book.* McGraw-Hill.

Hietanen, M., Erkinjuntti, T., & Huovinen, M. (2005). *Tunne muistisi- käytä, kehitä, kohenna.* WSOY.

Kump, P. (1999). *Breakthrough rapid reading.* Prentice Hall Press.

Lyman, P., & Varian, H. R. (2003). *How much information?* University of California, Berkeley.

Menecier, E. (1978). *Lectura Veloz.* Ediciones Baco.

Mishkin, M., & Appenzeller, T. (1987). *The anatomy of memory. Special report.* Scientific American, Inc.

Moidel, S. (1998). *Speed reading for business.* Barron's Educational Series.

Moller, C., Palmer, W., & Simpfendorfer, R. (1999). *Time manager for MS Outlook.* TMI Australia Pty Ltd.

Redway, K. (1991). *How to be a rapid reader.* National Textbook Company.

Rozakis, L. (1995). *Power reading.* MacMillan, Inc.

Rozakis, L., & Lichtenstein, E. (1995). *21st Century guide to increasing your reading speed.* Dell Publishing.

Russell, P. (1994). *The brain book.* Routledge Publishers.

Seiwert, L., Boethius, S., & Graichen, W. (1997). *Das 1 x 1 des zeitmanagement.* Gabal e. V.

Shenk, D. (1997). *Data smog—surviving the information glut.* Revised and Updated Edition. Harper Collins Publishers.

Smith, N. B. (1987). *Speed reading made easy.* CBS Inc./Prentice-Hall.

Articles

Allen, J., Bruss, J., & Damasio, H. (enero 2005). Estructura del cerebro humano. *Investigación y Ciencia,* 68–75.

Fields, D. (April 2004). The other half of the brain. *Scientific American,* 26–33.

Hintikka, K. (November 23, 2004). Elämän voi tallentaa joskus kiintolevylle. *Helsingin Sanomat.*

Ihanus, M. L. (February 7, 2002). Pikaluku tietokoneruudulta onnistuu. *IT-viikko,* 9.

Järvinen, P. (2003). Salaa sähköpostisi. *Tietokone, kesä-heinäkuu,* 105–106.

Kauppinen, J. (2002). Virus! *Mikrobitti, 3,* 54–61.

Liiten, M. (November 22, 2004). Mikä sen nimi nyt oli? *Helsingin Sanomat.*

Nieves, J. M. (March 18, 2005). The seven capital e-mail sins. *Sur in English,* 22.

Pajari, S. (January 2002). Näe hyvin näytöltä. *KotiPC,* 34–38.

Paukku, T. (November 16, 2004). Infoähky leviää maapallolla. *Helsingin Sanomat.*

Pulkkinen, M. (December 2002). Pysäytä roskaposti. *MikroPC,* 54–57.

Roth, G. (2004). The quest to find consciousness. *Scientific American Mind,* Special Edition, Volume 14, no. 1., 32–39.

Schakir, T. (March 28, 2002). Rasittavinta on Jatkuva kiire. *IT-viikko,* 21.

Sokala, H. (December 22, 2000). Kipu tulee myöhemmin. *Helsingin Sanomat.*

Ukkola, J. (2003). Sinulle on roskapostia. *Suomen Kuvalehti, 44,* 27–28.

Walker, L. (March 4, 2002). Web searchers get what advertisers pay for. *International Herald Tribune,* 13.

Wiio, O. (March 2001). Kolkuttaako omatunto? *Tietokone, 33.*

Web

How much info? http://www.sims.berkeley.edu, 2004.

Reading exercises, http://www.bbc.com, 2004.

The right viewing angle, http://www.ccohs.ca, 2000.

Safe office practice, www.openerg.com, 2005.